Our Amazing Cats

Short Tales of Feline Inspiration, Adventure and Humor

Compiled by R.J. Peters

Our Amazing Cats

Short Tales of Feline Inspiration,

Adventure and Humor

Compiled and Edited by RJ Peters

Dedication

This book is dedicated to anyone and everyone who has ever
loved a cat and knows just how amazing they all are.

Acknowledgements

Many thanks to the authors who contributed stories to this collection. Their accounts of the love and appreciation of the cats in their lives help others learn that cats are always amazing, whether or not they have done something unusual, whether or not they are physically challenged, and whether or not they are newsworthy. Here, in this book, they are all worthy of note and we are proud to present them to you for your enjoyment and appreciation of their special qualities.

Photos are by the respective authors and may not be copied. The cartoon graphic of Twister is by Christine, who can be found at this website: **http://fiverr.com/sweet_christine/make-cute-and-cuddly-animal**. The cover design is by Vikiana, who can be found at: **http://fiverr.com/vikiana/.**

A special thank you to Stu Bykofsky, renowned columnist with the Philadelphia Daily News, for taking time out of his busy schedule to write a story just for this book. See "Confessions of a Cat Lover." Also visit his website at **http://www.CatsAreSuperModels.com** and buy his book, Cats Are Supermodels.

Table of Contents

Introduction

Cats don't have to be extraordinary to be amazing. If you love cats, it's obvious that just being a cat is amazing.

For some, the amazement is tied to an unexpected behavior or talent, or perhaps a trait not usually attributed to cats. Anything they do, or look like, that isn't part of the stereotype is often called "amazing."

Cats who alert owners to a fire or an imminent seizure, for example, usually make the news as an amazing cat. Although this is more common with dogs, it appears some cats are able to tune in, too. I believe it's entirely possible, even probable, that cats are just as adept at detecting emergencies as dogs are, but humans are not very good at recognizing a cat's attempts to communicate an alert.

Cats are regarded as more subtle and such alerts may be missed more easily than those from dogs. Certainly, barking could be the biggest difference between dogs' and cats' methods of getting our attention.

So what is it that makes a cat amazing?

Is it something they do? Sure, that would qualify.

Is it a look or a physical attribute? Remember the cat last year with two faces? Yes, that's amazing.

Is it an accomplishment of some kind? Many cats have made the incredible journey to rejoin a family that moved to a new, but unfamiliar location hundreds of miles away.

However, amazement needn't be limited always to a newsworthy event or uncommon manifestation. We only need to take the time to appreciate the qualities that make these critters uniquely feline.

Cats can be wonderful, affectionate, intriguing, entertaining, comforting, talented escape artists, frustrating, challenging, and fun to play with, but sometimes they're just downright amazing for "whatever" reason. They may not get as much media attention or appreciation as dogs do, spotlighting their exploits, adventures and sometimes life-saving actions, but cats are just as capable of surprising us with their talents, and all we need to do is pay attention.

Lately, I've noticed that cats *are* starting to get more attention, as well as the credit they deserve, as journalists scramble for more and more human interest stories. Cats are now showing up in tales of adventure and intrigue, not to mention humor, all over the Internet. Especially popular now are kitten videos, and a recent study done in Japan revealed that watching such videos actually enhances one's ability to focus on a task.

So watch all the videos, read stories, and especially, spend extra time with your kitty. You both will benefit!

"Cats are connoisseurs of comfort." ~ James Herriot

Confessions of a Cat Lover

By Stu Bykofsky

Confession No. 1: I am not a cat lover.

I am a cat *admirer*, but not a cat "lover." Why?

Confession No. 2: I am afraid of my cat.

His name is Ashes. He is a bad boy. He bites and scratches.

I am South Korea; he is North Korea.

I am peaceful and democratic. He is aggressive, edgy, tyrannical, Isolated and spoiling for a fight.

Like South Korea, I give him food and treats and messages of fraternal affection. He sends back hairballs, hisses, baleful glares, needle-sharp teeth and razor-like claws.

I understand why he has issues. He is adopted, somehow dumped by his mother and sent to a shelter at the age of 5 weeks. That's pretty young to be motherless and abandoned, even for a cat.

I'm a "dog person," had dogs most of my life, so adopting this alien wasn't my idea. I know dogs, *really* well. I don't know cats, but now know they are very, very different.

"Credit" for the adoption goes to my then-girlfriend. (I'd call it blame, but I am a gentleman.)

She wanted a pet and our lives were too busy for a dog because of the care they require. She wheedled about getting a cat, which requires less attention, but I resisted and resisted. I finally agreed to take her to the Pennsylvania SPCA to "look" at what they had. Looking can't hurt – right?

Wrong.

While we were "looking," a furry black maniac came rocketing out of a cage full of cats and attached himself to her breasts like Velcro. I can relate to that, but....

She batted her eyes at me as I nonchalantly stared at the overhead fluorescent lights while humming "Another One Bites the Dust" very loudly, but it was to no avail.

The kitten was 5 weeks old and not ready to leave the shelter. "Come back next week," the attendant said, cheerfully.

That gave me a week to talk the girlfriend out of it. Being as she suffered from DSD (Designer Shoe Disorder) I thought I could get her friend Jimmy Choo to help me change her mind, from feline to 5-inch stilettos. "Forget the cat and get the pumps," I offered. No sale. She had fallen in love with the little kitty who had attached himself to her breasts.

A week trudged by on lead feet and the following Saturday we were back at the SPCA to accept the cat. Horror of horrors, my signature went on the adoption papers. A "dog person" soon would be the guardian of, and sharing quarters with, a c-a-t. No good will come of this, I (correctly) surmised.

Confession No. 3: Kittens are cuter than puppies, mostly because they don't poop on the rug.

I was amazed that the kitten learned – or already knew – how to do his business in a designated area, the litter box. That was amazing! Wow! No more early-morning or late-night walks in the park carrying a plastic bag for pooper scooping. Hey, maybe this won't be so bad.

The first time he used the litter box I was so proud I picked him up and hugged him. Mistake. He scratched me on the cheek.

Just an accident, I (wrongly) thought.

Confession No. 4: I learned I can't apply what I know about dog behavior to cat behavior.
When a dog wags his tail, you know he's friendly. When a cat switches her tail, I learned painfully, that's a warning.

When I tried to give Ashes a belly rub, I nearly lost a finger. That's another no-no – a dog-acceptable behavior that doesn't translate to cats.

When a dog looks into your eyes, he's communicating. When a cat looks into your eyes, it's a challenge. So I have learned to not look into my cat's eyes.

Great. Just freaking great.

Other warning signs are lowered ears, arched back, ears slanted back, ears flicking, expanded pupils, hissing.... You get the idea. There are so many cautions it's like living next door to a nuclear power plant.

Dogs pride themselves on being accessible. They are *with* you, always. Cats pride themselves on being aloof. With canines, it's *dog lovers*. With felines, it's *cat fanciers*. Fancy, my pants. Even *they* are aloof.

I acknowledge cats have the grace of a ballerina, the athleticism of a decathlete and the hunting prowess of Artemis, but warmth? I hear tales of affectionate cats, but I also hear tales of Elvis living in a condo in The Villages in Florida with Marilyn Monroe and JFK. (OK, OK. I have actually *seen* affectionate cats.)

Confession No. 5: Who could know "loves bites" is a form of affection?

As a kitten, when Ashes would "playfully" bite me, the girlfriend explained that is how cats show affection. Prior to Ashes' arrival, "love bites" was what I did to her.

"If that's how they show affection," I told the girlfriend, "there is something seriously wrong with their socialization skills."

I got a baleful glare from both the cat *and* the girlfriend.
The "loves bites" thing didn't go away with his kittenhood. Despite the fact that he has been cared for, loved and not abused in any way, Ashes bites and scratches without provocation, something no dog I lived with would ever do.

I got some good advice from a vet, to give him less affection, to make him want it more, and that worked pretty well, but I still approach him cautiously, and protect vulnerable body parts when he approaches me.

I have learned the warning signs and give him space.

It's been eight years. I have learned a lot about cat behavior, stuff you probably already knew, but which I do not want to discuss here because it depresses me.

The girlfriend is no longer in my life and it says something about her, and Ashes, that when she left she didn't take him with her. Maybe she was tired of puncture wounds.

Like South and North Korea, Ashes and I have a cold truce, an armed armistice, a suspicious civility. He is biting and scratching less, but that feral streak will never vanish. Something in a cat is forever wild, no matter how domesticated they are. That is why they deserve respect.

Confession No. 6: A cat is not a "pet."

You may live with a cat, but you don't "own" a cat. Nobody "owns" a cat. A cat is not a "pet" in the conventional sense of the customary relationship between a superior and inferior life form, as they used to say on *Star Trek*. You know the old line – dogs have guardians, cats have staff.

If you live with a cat, once you make peace with the idea that you are a servant, it will go better for you. It will be easier to maintain your sanity, dignity and sense of well-being.

Confession No. 7: I have made peace with the idea that I am Ashes' servant.

As he would say, "Meow."

Which translates to, "It's never too late to get smart, big boy. Now. . . feed me."

>^..^<

Stu Bykofsky is an American journalist and columnist for the Philadelphia Daily News. He has been a columnist since 1987 and is one of the most widely read journalists in the city. Why he refers to dogs as "he" and cats as "she" is fully explored in his book, Cats Are Supermodels. For more information, visit **http://www.CatsAreSupermodels.com.**

"Cats can be cooperative when something feels good, which, to a cat, is the way everything is supposed to feel as much of the time as possible."
~ Roger Caras

Twister's Adventure - The Cat That Pulled a Rock Across Alaska

By R.J. Peters

Twister started life in 1994 as the runt of a litter in a feral cat colony behind a friend's house. My friend made sure they all had plenty to eat, but that was the extent of concern for their welfare. While further care would have been optimal, at least the colony was not in danger of imminent extermination, which is more common in most communities.

Originally we called the tiny tuxedo kitten "that twisted neck cat" because her head was permanently rotated to one side, known as a wry neck when it happens to people, and was probably due to a birth injury. This turned out to be a lucky break for her, though, because all the healthy, active cats were viewed simply as a group, sort of an entity whose moving parts were a bunch of cats.

Nobody really stood out, until I spotted the little one trying to eat. With great difficulty, not only because she had to wriggle in to the dish through a crowd of hungry and stronger siblings who kept pushing her out of the way, but because she also had to get into a position that allowed her to grab a bite here and there. I knew she would not survive long with those odds, so I captured her and took her home.

However, she was a very strong kitten and proved to be a challenge to snatch. In those days, I didn't have any cages, pet taxis or traps, so a large cardboard box had to serve for transportation to the house. She almost escaped many times, though the box was six or seven times her height. She sure could jump! Since there were no shelters or rescue programs in our area at the time, and I was not equipped to save them all, I had to have faith that the colony would be OK, as long as no one bothered them and my friend continued to feed them.

I estimated Twister's age by the growth and development of her litter mates...about 8 weeks...because she was so small she appeared much younger. With individual and special care, she became tame very quickly, and without having to struggle to eat, she grew fast, though she never really caught up with the others. I don't think she ever exceeded 7 pounds her entire life, but she grew strong and healthy and was soon ready to be spayed and vaccinated and got a clean bill of health.

She joined my little family of 3 cats and played them to exhaustion every day, which gave me an idea.

While her neck condition improved a little on its own over time, I decided to use my knowledge and skills as a chiropractor to see if I could help her recover more fully and avert a permanent, lifelong disability. Massage and trigger points helped, but it was the exercise routines I came up with that proved most effective. I devised games-as-exercise that strengthened the muscles opposing those responsible for her malpositioned head and neck.

By the time she was a year old, she appeared completely normal and only we who knew her well could detect the slight twist that remained. Occasionally, someone would comment that she appeared to be listening for something because her head was cocked ever so slightly to one side, but she had to be sitting still long enough to notice it. At her age, that was pretty seldom. She was a very active kitten!

And then we decided to take a vacation to Alaska. We planned to drive our camping van and spend a month exploring the cities, towns and wilderness areas. But what about Twister? We couldn't leave her alone that long, and we didn't think she would do well in a foster home. Boarding her was completely out of the question because she would go crazy if she couldn't move around and play. I remember, as a child, my family took a 3-week vacation one summer and my parents boarded our Siamese cat. On our return, we learned that she was close to death. The strain of being caged that long was too much for her, and if we hadn't returned when we did, she would have died. To prevent that sort of consequence, we simply included Twister in our plans and made room for her and her things in the van.

The cats left behind were cared for by a hired house- and pet-sitter, which worked out very well as they were older and probably welcomed the relief from their new, rambunctious "little sister."

The first two days on the road were frightening and stressful for Twister, but she was young, full of curiosity and learned to adapt. In no time, she was happily darting around in motel rooms every night, inventing games of her own, and was mesmerized by the world passing swiftly by as she sat in her "car seat" by a window in the van during the day.

Once we reached Canada, we started looking for campgrounds instead of motels because it was less expensive and because the weather was spectacular and we wanted to be outdoors. In Alaska, this was even more important due the huge increase in lodging costs. Also, the scenery was so incredible we wanted to be immersed in it.

21

But staying in campgrounds brought up the biggest problem of all that we hadn't thought of: How can we keep Twister safe? We didn't want to leave her locked up inside the van while we were enjoying hikes and campfires and outdoor activities. She could only watch us having fun from her perch by the window which certainly must have been distressing and confusing. She was still a kitten and needed the exercise!

So we trained her to walk on a leash. That worked well for a while, but in just a few days we realized that wasn't the best answer either. Someone had to be holding the leash all the time and walking her. This preoccupied one of us and precluded all activities, such as hiking, shopping and simply relaxing around the fire. So I got the bright idea to tie her leash to a rock. We had already learned you can't tether a cat to a tree; they run around it and become impossibly tangled, or try to run up the tree and yank themselves rudely back down once the end of the leash is reached.

Tethering to a picnic table was worse, and leaving her "caged" in the van was making her crazy. But the rock turned out to be absolutely brilliant....we thought. And it was, at first. We found a craggy specimen at the foot of a mountain in Skagway, which turned out to be perfect for tying a leash on it. The rough bumps prevented the cord from sliding off, and the cat could walk in circles without becoming tangled. She finally could be outdoors with us as we cooked and relaxed at our campsites.

Over the next week or so, we noticed how strong she was becoming. She began dragging the rock behind her and was thus able to expand her territory without going too far or running away. We had a good laugh one evening as we noted how she appeared to be in training to be a "sled cat."

Then one afternoon, at a new campsite, she decided to graduate to a whole new level of rock-dragging. She now could run! Not fast, but she was stepping right along, and with a hint of worry, we said, "We're going to need a bigger rock."

When we located one and approached her to make the switch, she suddenly darted away and took off across a city park near the campground where we had parked. She was bounding along faster than either of us expected, but surely she had not expected that she would be "chased" by that bouncing rock! Naturally, we ran after her, hoping to snatch the rope before anything horrible happened, like running into traffic!

Just as she reached the sidewalk, with the street just on the other side of it, she ran to one side of a light pole and her rock bounced behind her and veered off to the other side of the pole.

We stopped in our tracks and watched for the inevitable. As the rope wrapped around the pole from the opposing velocities of rock and cat, we felt sick about an impending collision.

It all took only a few split seconds, and suddenly, there she was, snugged up against the pole, sitting on top of the rock.

Horrified, I gently removed the now terrified one year old kitten and carried her back to our campsite, where we sat with her, inside the van, comforting her.

The next day, incredibly, she was ready to explore the world yet again, apparently having totally forgotten the events of the day before.

We tied her to the new, bigger rock, and we moved along on our journey with the tentative belief that surely she would not be able to overcome her new "ball and chain."

As it turned out, she never was able to run like a deer again, but she did become stronger and was soon able to drag her new rock anyway. As small as she was, one would think a 15 pound rock would hold down a 7 pound cat. But she had reached her limit, as all body builders must, and even learned to accept her situation. We made sure to take her on regular walks whenever we stopped anywhere, and she dutifully stayed within her boundary created by the length of the leash. It was only in motel rooms, which we decided to use once a week to give her some "room" to move more freely, that she could dart about and get some fun exercise and play games.

Just as we thought this story was done, another hair-raising event happened in Anchorage, in a motel room, and it taught us another lesson.

We needed the time in town ourselves, to regroup, clean out the van, do laundry, and enjoy modern life for a few days. Twister immediately made herself at home for our three-day vacation within our vacation.

That first night, after she tired of leaping between the beds, she darted under one and stayed there. We assumed she was napping and would appear on our bed later when we had retired for the night. When she didn't show up to sleep on us, we became concerned. We looked under the beds and any furniture she could squeeze under. No sign of our kitty.

Now we were really worried. Had she gotten out? If so, how? Reviewing our activities, we established that no one had opened the door all evening. When I checked the windowsill to see if she was resting there, behind the curtains, I discovered the window was open and there was no screen!

Oh no! That was it! She had gone out the window, but when?

Here it was, 10 p.m. at a busy intersection, and our black cat was lost in the black of night.

We walked around the area for over an hour and left notice with every business that was still open. We set out dishes of food. We explored the bushes with flashlights. We even looked along the busy boulevard for signs of a motionless object the size of a cat.

Finding nothing, we hung our heads and headed back to bed, destined to stare at the ceiling all night. I left the window open for the breeze. Why close it now?

When I remembered she was wearing a collar and tags, I also realized how useless they were. Her tags only carried our home address and phone number a thousand miles away. It had never occurred to me to put updated "vacation tags" on her collar with our cell phone number (a novelty in those days, but still useful).

After an eternity of worry and kicking myself for letting this happen, there was a soft thump on the bed. It was 3 a.m. I bolted upright in bed and flipped on the lamp. It was Twister! We could not believe it. She had found her way "home" to a completely strange motel and jumped in through the right window.

We were ecstatic and I closed the window, first thing. Then we focused on Twister, who totally relished the attention. She had no marks on her, she was clean, and she was not limping or favoring any body parts. She was just fine! We regarded this as a stroke of luck that she not only survived but had brought herself back to us.

We took Twister with us on a few more vacation trips over the next few years, equipped with vacation ID tags, but as she matured, it was clear she didn't enjoy these journeys as much anymore. She is the most traveled cat I have known, though certainly other cats have done more. We took Twister to all four corners of the United States on our travels.

She passed away in July, 2010, and is very missed around here. Her life was eventful and full of love and adventure, as all cats deserve. She was 16. Perhaps she would have lived longer if not for her difficult beginning in life. We'll never know if the neurological damages were responsible for a shorter lifespan. She had gone totally, stone deaf by the time she was 10, but it didn't stop her from enjoying life. And it didn't stop us from enjoying her.

Twister at 16

>^..^<

Dr. R.J. Peters, a retired health care professional, started an animal shelter in 2002, rescuing approximately 1,000 cats since then. She has published numerous books, ebooks and articles on animal care based on personal experience, research and advice from the experts.

Visit her website at: **http://theproblemcat.com** and sign up for the biweekly newsletter, The Kitty Times.

"Cats are smarter than dogs. You can't get eight cats to pull a sled through snow." ~ Jeff Valdez

Baxter

By Anna Balsamo

With right eye swollen and oozing, and body limply laying on a
log with barely a breath left in him – that is how we found him
that sticky, humid day in July. It was a miracle he was even alive.
Just three weeks before we saw him with the rest of the litter
hanging on his mother's breast. But not this day. This day he was
abandoned, left gasping for life all on his own.

"Anna," screamed my husband, "come quickly! There's a kitten in
our yard. He looks very sick. We've got to help him."

I scrambled to remove the rubber gloves from my hands (I was
washing the bathroom), and raced down the stairs and out the
back door.

"Where is it?" I cried.

"Over there. Lying on that log," answered my husband.

There he was (of course, we didn't know he was a he then!)
looking so weak and feeble. He didn't even try and run from me. I

gently picked him up, wrapped him in an old towel and placed him in an empty box my husband had retrieved.

"Now what?" I asked my husband. "What do I do with him? I've never owned a cat before and you're allergic to them."

"Well, I know that, but we have to do something. We just can't let it die."

So off I went to call the local vet. The same one we had used for our dog, George, when he was still with us.

The young lady on the phone took all the information down and then asked me, "Don't bring him in here and spend money to get him looked at if you aren't going to keep him." So I ran outside and my husband emphatically said, "Yes," we could keep him.

A few hours later he was being seen by the vet. She quickly diagnosed him with conjunctivitis and prescribed an ointment for his eye. Then she turned and said, "You know, I don't want you to get your hopes up high. Most kittens this small – and he is very, very skinny right now – most times they don't make it. I doubt he will even make it to Monday. But if he does (that's when we found out "it" was a "he"), bring him back and we will do a thorough checkup on him. In any case, he has to eat something! Have you given him anything?"

"No. Not yet. I never took care of a cat before and he looked pretty pathetic. I didn't know what to do and just waited to see you before I did anything," I answered her.

Well, here's some canned food. Mix it with water so he will be able to eat it. Give him lots of food as often as he wants to eat along with water. He must eat or he will die!" she said very firmly.

We tried and tried to get him to eat, but couldn't. He just didn't have enough strength in him. But then, thankfully, our son's girlfriend put a bit of food on her hand and he began to gently lick it up – though only minute pieces at a time. Success at last!

During that first weekend, we held him almost constantly and fed him as often as he would eat. He was so tiny he fit in the palm of my hand! He was nearly all fur, specifically charcoal gray fur with white front feet and back paws. Mittens and boots I think they call them. His belly was all white, too, making him look a bit like a tuxedo cat.

He was pitiful to look at with his right eye swollen shut and oozing from the corners, and it was difficult to get the ointment in his eyes. But the little guy, who by now we had named Baxter, was very cooperative.

I have to admit I was a nervous wreck. I was hosting a huge party the day after we found him with well over 40 people and there was a lot to do around our home to get ready for it. The whole time I was preparing and cleaning I was thinking and praying for our little Baxter and wondering if he would eat enough to get a bit stronger. Thankfully, one of my younger cousins was glad to pitch in and help me with Baxter. She tended to him while I was busy serving my guests. She was so sweet and gentle with him. Once I checked in on them and there he lay in her lap while she was reading to him! How grateful I was for her help. It didn't seem to bother her that he looked so pathetic and weak. She was glad to love him and cuddle him.

By Monday morning, I knew he would be okay. I didn't need the doctor to tell me that. He looked stronger and was eating much better and now from a small bowl.

When I brought him back to the vet, she was amazed at his recovery. She ran tests on him and did all sorts of things to get him up to speed and kept marveling at his miraculous state. She told me to come back in a month for his rabies vaccine and to continue his eye ointment. And that was that.

Baxter continued to grow, and by August he had become quite a handful. I didn't know kittens were so active! I was constantly online asking questions and finding answers to all my kitten questions. My queries ranged from the broad, "How do you play with cats?" to the self preserving, "How do you keep them from scratching you?"

But his eyes weren't any better; in fact, the infection had spread to the other eye despite my best efforts.

Then one Friday night in the middle of August, my husband and I were out to dinner with friends and our son phoned to say, "Mom, I don't think Baxter can see. I'm playing with him using that new laser toy and he isn't following the light. Not at all."

My eyes welled up with tears as I relayed this information to my husband. We were a bit surprised because it didn't seem like he couldn't see. He had no trouble moving about the house and found his food bowl without incident and even used his new litter box without a problem.

The next morning I phoned the vet and we brought him in. The doctor probed and probed with his little flashlight instrument, then turned and said to us, "I have some bad news I am sorry to say; I think he is blind. I will give you a few moments to think about what you want to do."

He said cats can live very well with blindness. They have such a good sense of hearing and smell that it shouldn't be much of a problem, but that we could also decide to put him to sleep if we felt that would be best.

Well, by now my tears were flowing freely and once we were alone my husband turned and asked me, "Well, Hon, what do you think we should do? Whatever you want is fine with me." But tears were in his eyes, too. You see, we had both grown to love our little kitten. He was now part of our family. How could we get rid of him?

"Well, if he were a little boy with such a problem we wouldn't get 'rid' of him, would we?" I sobbed. The two of us sat in that examining room crying and hanging onto Baxter for dear life. A decision was made. We would keep him. The doctor seemed happy, but surprised. He even congratulated us for our care and concern for this little guy. It was then that I asked if the ointment could be switched to drops instead. He agreed. We would bring him back in a month.

Three times a day I gave him his drops and by now it was a chore trying to catch him! He was getting tired of being man-handled so often by me. As the month went by I noticed his eyes were starting to clear up a bit. Then one night, my husband was playing with him and decided to try the laser light again. Baxter hesitated, and then went chasing after it!

Shouts of hurray and halleluiah could probably be heard from across the street we were so happy. Tears were once more shed and poor Baxter was hugged and hugged before being put down again – much to his relief!

The vet was amazed at his recovery (again!) and prescribed more eye drops in the hopes he would continue on the path to wholeness.

And he did. Baxter is now over a year old and lying at my feet as I type these words. He has no trouble seeing, and is now getting different eye drops (just once a day now) to help heal the scars on his retina.

I guess he thinks that's just what all cats have to go through in life. Part of the routine: eat, drink, jump in the litter box and get eye drops everyday!

He doesn't seem to mind. I guess that's because he knows he's well loved. And he is!

>^..^<

Anna Balsamo, wife, mother, cat lover and author. Find more of my articles on **www.heartsongworship.org.** Follow the link on the left under my name.

"A kitten is the most irresistible comedian in the world. Its wide-open eyes gleam with wonder and mirth. It darts madly at nothing at all, and then, as though suddenly checked in the pursuit, prances sideways on its hind legs with ridiculous agility and zeal." ~ Agnes Repplier

My Lost Love, Beaster

By Christine Houde

I was five years old the first time I picked up a cat. Because I didn't know what I was doing, didn't know the correct way to pick up a cat, my hand got very badly scratched. The scratches got badly infected and subsequently left scars on the heel of my right hand. My mother said I was completely cat crazy ever since.

When Beaster came into my life, I was involved in breeding and showing Tonkinese cats. He was born into my hands. He was one of ten kittens from two litters that were born in my guest room. I didn't take particular note of him except to see that he was a bit smaller than the others. He seemed healthy. He was a runt. But what a sociable runt! When the kittens got old enough to socialize, prospective "parents" were invited in to sit on the floor and visit with them. I generally encouraged people to let their forever kitten choose them. Beaster was always out there, jumping in people's laps, climbing to their shoulders, asking, "Are you my new mama, papa?" Because of his size, I guess, he was largely ignored.

I didn't worry about it because he was always the first "piggy to the trough" and the last one to leave—a very enthusiastic eater! Then one day I noticed that he was considerably smaller than the others and I caught him at the litter box having a bowel movement I found very alarming. The consistency was ok but the color was shockingly off. It was a kind of grayish clay color.

I whipped that boy into a carrier and took off for the doctor's office. The vet wanted to put him down right away having decided that Beaster was suffering from a serious enzyme deficiency that was causing some kind of organ failure. He stayed at the vet's for a couple of days getting sicker—stopped eating and got lethargic. Even so, some man who was visiting his own sick cat fell in love with Beaster and told me if he ever recovered he'd give me whatever price I named for him.

The vet continued to advocate euthanasia but I didn't want to give up yet so I took Beaster to a specialty clinic. There the doctor told me they thought he had a liver shunt and wanted to do a liver biopsy. I asked if it could possibly be anything else. He said it might be some kind of opportunistic protozoa that was "stealing" Beaster's nutrients. He suggested we try treating it systematically with a drug.

Every day I got up and went downstairs, I never knew if I would find that little guy dead or alive. I had to force feed him food and water. I had to clean his bottom. He slept on my chest and stomach all the time, except when I had to care for the others. My husband was out of the country at the time. I just lay on the sofa and held him. I was afraid to get him very wet in case of chilling him so he got kind of messy. At that time his name was Pigpen. A groomer friend of mine told me she could bathe and dry him keeping him warm the whole time and I jumped at it. He really seemed to feel better all cleaned up.

After four days of this, he finally began to eat on his own and I knew he would recover. We never did know exactly what was wrong. He was still very small. Packed away with my things in Florida is a photo of him next to his sister Sally at the age of 4 months. She was 2 ½ times his size! I couldn't be sure that there wasn't something genetically wrong with him and the vets thought he wouldn't live more than 5 years. So, I decided to neuter and keep him. And I'm so glad I did! After that illness, he was never sick again for over 8 years—not so much as a sniffle or upset stomach!

He developed into the most wonderful cat I've ever had! He never met a living being he didn't welcome gladly. New cats or kittens coming into the house greeted with a bath instead of hisses or growls. And, of course, he loved people!!!

When my queens had kittens, they trusted him to baby sit and he would get into their nest boxes, curl himself around their babies, bathing and cuddling them. He was such an uncle! And as the kittens got older and more active he played with them endlessly—gently.

A breeder friend of my brought me two 3 month old kittens to babysit for a couple days because she didn't have room. A few evenings later, when she came to pick them up, she put the kittens in the zippered carrier and we stood talking for a few minutes. Then she secured everything, took them out to her car and left.

Ten minutes later, I realized I hadn't seen Beaster. I was frantic when I couldn't find him anywhere. I was terrified he'd gotten out when my friend left. We were living in semi-rural Florida at the time and it is definitely not safe outside for cats! Finally, out of desperation I called my friend and begged her to pull off the road and check the carrier. Sure enough, my Beaster had gotten into the carrier and was cuddled up with the two little boys. My friend said she thought it felt kind of heavy when she left my house...

Beaster and I were devoted to one another. He wasn't just my 'cat.' He was my friend and companion. Oh, yes, he loved my husband, too, but Beaster was truly mine and I was his. And he was smart! He learned what certain words meant to the point where Joe and I had to say them backwards so as not to get Beaster excited. "Play" became "Yalp" and "toys" became "syots." He knew where the toys were kept, and by toys I mean the teasers, and he knew how to tell me he wanted to play. He would call me and "haunt" the drawer or try to open it and the closet door—succeeding when he was persistent enough. He could come and tell me when he was hungry. He could tell me lots of things in ways different enough that I could understand what it was he wanted—food, love, play, in/out of the bedroom. He had some subtle facial expressions, too. One that I've wondered about lately is a wrinkling on his head between his ears—was it a headache? Pain? Fear?

And could that boy kiss! We loved to smooch. I used to say he was exfoliating my face! But as part of his ardor, he would also nip my nose and chin. Those nose nips were painful until realized that I shouldn't pull away. It was the pulling away that made him chomp down. Most cats knead, I guess; we call it making "happy feet." Beaster kneaded two ways—one was just regular but the other was distinctly reminiscent of a baby nursing—head down and with a definite, faster, rhythmic beat.

He only got out once--when we moved into our apartment in Vista, California. One of us didn't close the screen door all the way and he took off. Luckily I noticed pretty quickly and after a few frantic minutes running around the community and calling him, he answered me from the pool area. When I ran over to catch him, instead to taking off for further tastes of freedom, he ran right to me.

The last two recessions destroyed our economic well being and now we live on SSI. We moved from a 4,000 square foot house into a one bedroom apartment. We have had a hard time adjusting to the change in our circumstances. Beaster has been my comfort and my sunshine. He has always been that but lately more so. I am well aware how profoundly he loved me and tried to care for me.

Beaster was a great traveler! He flew across country with us twice. Four years ago, a couple of my husband's associates rented an RV and we took a trip to research mines in Arizona and New Mexico. We took Beaster with us and he had a ball! He found the litter box and his food and water right away on his exploration tour of the RV. He sat in everybody's laps; loved to sit on the table and look out the window as we drove. He really wanted to sit on the dashboard but obviously we couldn't let that happen. He enriched everyone's trip. He was such a good companion!

He slept with me, stayed in my lap a lot. He used to pretend to sneak up and surprise me by going around to the back of my recliner and jumping onto the arm of the chair from behind it. I always pretended I was surprised—for his benefit.

Over the years I made up three silly little songs about him. One of them ended, "...kiss me once, kiss me twice, kiss me again because it's so nice..." I'd bend over when I came to that part and he'd jump up and bump noses on 'once...twice...[and]...nice.' The last song I made up had sweet loving words but the melody (I borrowed from an old swashbuckler movie) was sad and mournful.

Two months before he was diagnosed with Hypertrophic Cardiomyopathy, I suddenly felt compelled to take pictures of him. I'm not a photographer; I don't take pictures; but I went out and bought two throwaway cameras and filled them up with pictures. I got him cuddling with me in bed; kissing me; laying his cheek against mine and many other photos that captured who he was. Looking back, when I consider the sad song and the photos, I wonder if some part of me knew I was close to losing him.

We lived with that diagnosis, in desperate love and fear for 10 months. Every morning the first thing I did was look for him to make sure he was still alive. Every time I left the apartment, I looked for him first thing for the same reason. Every time I had to increase his Lasix dose, I went to pieces. I had to have him put to sleep on March 25th and it was the hardest thing I've ever done in my life. I feel him everywhere in our apartment; once I felt him brush against my leg and once I heard him jump up from behind my chair. His physical absence feels like being hit by a sharp painful silence that is absolute and my world seems somewhat dimmer.

As he got older, first passing that 5 year benchmark, then onward without ever getting sick again, I began to believe he would live until around age 20, which is the normal life span for healthy Tonks. Though I never took him for granted, I came to count on his presence in my life.

I'm in that stage where I'm terrified I will never love again but know I will need to. It's hard to imagine ever having a cat as loving as my lost Beaster.

This year, 2012, on August 15th, my darling boy would have been 12 years old.

"It was not I who was teaching my cat to gather rosebuds, but (he) who was teaching me."

~ *Irving Townsend*

Flirty Foxy

By Nancy Dutton

Outside my picture window on a sunny June day, I heard a loud, "Queg-queg-queg, quawk-quawk-quawk." A large magpie bird flew over my cat Foxy, who thought her grey hair and striped tail camouflaged her in the grass, an unseen warrior in hiding. True to her cat nature, she showed no surprise as the bird came perilously close to her head.

Foxy looked side to side, out the corners of her eyes, as if maybe she heard something.

Her eyes nonchalantly said, "Nah, just back to relaxing for me. Oh, what a beautiful day!" Although Foxy ignored the bird, I knew she was aware that it was trying to intimidate her. *A sly little fox today*, I thought.

I named her Foxy because as a kitten, she looked like a fox. Her jaw line was thinner than her forehead, her little ears perched on top of her small head, and she had a tapered snout. I loved that big, fluffy tail. Oh, what a Foxy Lady, as I sang the popular song from the hippie era.

The magpie flew past the cat and the blue spruce tree nearby. Annoyed that Foxy did not notice the fierce danger to her life, the black-and-white bird circled back around in preparation to dive-bomb Foxy again.

Growing a little anxious about the safety of my precious cat, I grabbed the patio-door handle, in case a sudden rescue was necessary. I nicknamed the bird Maggie Magpie, not knowing if it was male or female. Apparently, there is no way to tell the sex of a magpie, even if you are a bird expert or ornithologist.

Swoosh, zoom, varoom . . .the screaming bird pilot flew close to Foxy's head. Again, Foxy looked around as if nothing had happened. She folded her paws in front of her chest, signaling she was comfortable and might stay outside awhile on this glorious day. But I was certain that Foxy, in typical cattitude, really saw the bird and was in complete control of the situation.

Two times Maggie missed striking Foxy. Now I felt slightly comforted that this noisy bird might not harm my cat. My hand eased off the door handle, as I took a ringside seat at the window. Foxy and I were both entertained with this flirty tug-of-war game of scare and dare, or is it scare and beware? Each participant thought they would win, but only one could be the champion. Free entertainment in my own backyard is a great stress reliever, too!

Hearing my laughter at the outdoor events, my husband sat down by me for the next round. Compelled to discover all possible details, he searched the internet for information on magpies. Apparently they live in the western part of North America, a very common bird that is a member of the crow family called Corvidae (for those who want to know). The website says magpies are a form of songbird, but I do not like the grating sound they make. To me, a songbird sings a sweet melody, music to my ears. This bird had an aggravating caw, not soothing to my soul.

My husband continued his research while I enjoyed watching the outdoor show. He announced that magpies have a black bill, head, chest, wings and long tail, with white bellies, shoulders and white patches on the wings and a wingspan of 22 to 24 inches. I could see that. No need to do research, in my mind, when it was obvious what the bird looked like.

Back to the show . . .Maggie swooped low as she came toward Foxy. *"Surely this will scare and intimidate this ignorant cat!"* thought Maggie. Down Maggie flew toward her target. "Queg-queg-queg, quawk-quawk-quawk."

Another miss! Whew, that was close. We smiled like proud parents as an unfazed Foxy licked her paws, cleaned her face and basked in the sun as if to say, *"Another uneventful day in paradise."* We could almost see a smile on her face, as she delighted in conquering the magpie. *"That noisy gnat flying in the air, I will not let the negative energy change my day or make me feel bad. Doesn't this irritant have something better to do than to pester me?"*

Boy, don't we humans wish we could deflect the everyday annoyances in our lives and not let the negative people and things get us down? Why can't we just continue on with our happy days and be content to enjoy life, whatever it may bring, like Foxy? She let nothing stand in the way of her peace, love and joy. She knew not to take life's curves too seriously. Wish I could be that happy with my life the way it is and laugh a little more.

On and on the game continued. Maggie Magpie repeatedly did fly-bys and circled back to do it all over again. Foxy continued to remain peaceful and undaunted by the bird's actions.

A few minutes passed by as I enjoyed the snow-capped mountain view. Suddenly, Foxy the Conqueror sat up and decided it was time to quit letting this silly bird be frustrated by trying to hurt her. She scurried back to the house without even a meow as the magpie flew off to look for more rewarding mischief. Ah, another feline victory.

We opened the door as our proud child came inside the house. We greeted her with congratulatory rubs as she strutted in and "rabbit-footed" her favorite mouse toy, showing off her prowess and superiority. Then Foxy walked over to her food bowl, where a favorite treat was instantly dropped into the bowl, a fine reward for her natural ability to remain in peace, love and joy under adverse circumstances.

>^..^<

Nancy Dutton is a freelance writer who has published the Book of Animal Poetry. She has written articles that have appeared in a variety of publications. Nancy writes customized poems and haikus and has taught classes on how to write haiku to children. She has written hundreds of poems, haiku, songs, stories about animals and children, plus inspirational stories about life. Visit her website at **www.nancysworld.us** and read some of her poems, haikus and articles. Her book is available at **http://www.amazon.com/Book-of-Animal-Poetry-ebook/dp/B006H6Y5FC**

When not writing, Nancy likes to hike, paint, photograph animals, travel, and ride motorcycles. She also spends time with family, friends and her two cats.

"I love cats because I enjoy my home; and little by little, they become its visible soul." *~ Jean Cocteau*

Radar, Best Cat Ever

By R.J. Peters

Cats like Radar don't come along very often. His extraordinary intelligence must account for his survival as a stray in a very small town in a rural area where strays are usually shot, not gathered up by animal control and impounded. So when neighbors called to tell me he was about to be shot, I knew I had to save him.

He had no future, with local authorities gunning for him. He would not be going to a shelter, unless it was mine.

No one knows how long he lived on the street, but he learned how to survive by convincing nice humans to look out for him and locating food wherever he could, though his condition indicated that didn't happen every day. However, inveterate cat haters kept him on his toes and on the move to avoid a final confrontation, and now his days were numbered.

He was extremely thin when I rescued him – almost emaciated – and his long fur was severely matted and had to be shaved off. He was so thin, we even had to wait until he was healthy enough to be neutered and vaccinated. The vet guessed he was at least 8, possibly 12, but most likely around 10 years old. I think we settled on the average, there.

What a pathetic picture he made until he recovered his beautiful coat and reached a healthy weight... around 17 pounds...after a year at the shelter. He dutifully accepted cage life, hopping out on request for morning and evening cleanings, and jumping back in when I told him, "Your room is ready, sir."

When I changed the environment from cages to an open shelter model, Radar went along with the new arrangement as if it had been his idea, often comforting or disciplining other cats who needed help getting used to it. He then took over the job of welcoming new arrivals and giving them their orientation tours.

It didn't take me long to realize just how smart he was, and I started taking him with me to events and speaking engagements where animals were allowed. Whenever he was on the agenda, our shelter always got the best donations. He knew how to "work a room," that's for sure.

He became so popular that adoption requests increased – for him. But I never met just the right person for him and eventually took him off the list. I decided the best home for him was mine! He went home with me one day and became my personal cat. I still took him to public activities as the shelter "spokescat" and he continued to win hearts and open wallets every time. He seemed to enjoy public life and I appointed him the official public relations 'rep' for the shelter. He put up with elderly people hugging him a little too hard at nursing homes, and children holding him awkwardly during children's story hour at the library and other events. He seemed to understand that it was his job to help people understand the needs of cats.

Then, when the shelter had to close, we moved to an old, remote farm and took all the "leftover" animals with us. Radar quickly assessed the new location and took charge of everyone's activities, including the dogs. No one messed with Radar, or he reminded them who was top cat. He could be tough when needed, but managed to do so in a firm but gentle and understanding way.

I will always miss him sleeping next to me and purring. His best "talent" was an apparent realization that his sharp claws hurt human skin, and he never extended his claws when he was kneading on my lap.

With Radar, it was hard to think of this behavior as kneading because his technique was somewhat unique. He used all four feet and literally marched in place, stepping lively. He wasn't even close to "making biscuits." Whatever one wishes to call it, I loved it. It was quite a nice massage! He seemed to know how much I enjoyed it, too, as he would often go for as long as an hour, checking my face for signs of approval every so often.

He began losing weight that year, almost imperceptibly under his long fur, but in time, it was obvious whenever I picked him up. He was never sick, so there was nothing the vet had to say, other than to be sure he was eating well. And that was never a problem! He wasn't even choosy. But one day he just sniffed the dish and walked away. Then he darted out when I went outside...and disappeared. He'd done this before, so I wasn't worried. He always came to me when I called, so I figured he was surveying his kingdom and would return. He did.

But he didn't come inside when invited. I had to lift him off the dog's bed by the front door and carry him in. Then I knew. I could feel it, sense it somehow, that he was saying good bye.

I set up a large basket with sheepskins in it for him to relax on, and he curled up in there, right where I put him.

I kept him with me all evening, and just after midnight, May 6, 2010, he lifted his head to look at me and let out a long sigh, settling down on his soft pads. I petted him and thanked him for being in my life and cried softly for a long time, lying on the floor beside him. He was 18.

Good bye Radar... I don't know when the heartache will end, but I will never forget...the best cat, ever.

>^..^<

45

Radar

"As anyone who has ever been around a cat for any length of time well knows, cats have enormous patience with the limitations of the human kind. "

~ Cleveland Amory

Goldie

By Fritz Owens

We lived in a house on Robert St. in New Orleans from about 1967 through 1974. My wife and the kids found this female cat with kittens someplace and we kept one and gave the rest, including the mother, away. We called the cat Goldie because she had golden hair as a kitten. As she got older, the ends of the hair started to turn that gray and black typical of a feline domestic shorthair. However, if you pushed the hair aside so you could see her skin, it was still gold colored next to her skin.

Goldie was an exceptionally smart cat. She lived in the house but went outside when she wanted to. To start with she would meow at the door to get in and then would push at the door when no one responded. Eventually she learned to stand to the left side of the door, grab the door with her left paw and pull it open far enough to get inside. We had no air conditioning so we left the door unlocked in the back all the time except at night. We never thought much about it because Goldie coming in and going out of the house was just the normal state of things.

Then Aunt Marie came to visit us briefly from California on her trip to Florida. I had to tell the kids (just the two of them then) who were about six and five, that they had to keep Goldie out of the house while Aunt Marie was there. Poor Aunt Marie was petrified by cats - couldn't even bear to watch one cross the street without shuddering. So we were successful in keeping Goldie out by locking the screen door in the back and keeping the front door closed, which had no screen - for a while.

Now, I think most everyone knows that cats seem to sense when someone doesn't like them. I experienced too many situations where the only answer was the cat had to know a particular person didn't like cats. One of those situations I didn't even know a student of mine didn't like cats. So Goldie went around the house a couple of times meowing and banging on the back door screen and then apparently lay down next to the front door and waited.

While we were entertaining Aunt Marie in the living room, Helen and Nani came through and told us that they were going outside to play on the swing set. I told them to be sure and not let Goldie into the house. The next thing I know, a gray streak races in, jumps to the back of the sofa and BANG! right into Aunt Marie's lap, a quick leap to the floor and Goldie races off to the kitchen leaving Aunt Marie with her hair standing on end. I was certain that poor lady was having a stroke! It was all we could do to keep from falling on the floor laughing about it but we managed to keep quiet while trying to soothe Aunt Marie.

Thankfully, she survived and after she left, it became part of the Owens family history and their cats. We have enjoyed many a good laugh about that situation since it really was hysterical. In 1974 we moved from that house since we now had four girls and there wasn't enough room. We ended up moving to a two story double on Carrollton Ave. and leasing both sides, which gave us six bedrooms upstairs and a living room, dining room, kitchen on one side and my studio, office and utility room on the other. The difference here was the kitchen door opened the opposite from Robert Street.

Poor Goldie, the four years we lived there she never did figure out how to open the door because it was situated right next to a wall on the porch that was part of the water heater closet. Instead, she pushed very vigorously on the door to make a banging noise and someone would open the door to let her in. One night, after I got off work, Rene, the bandleader and I were sitting at the kitchen table discussing our upcoming recording session. It was three o'clock in the morning when there came a knocking at the kitchen door. Rene looked at the clock and said, "Who could that be knocking on your door at three in the morning?" and I said, "Oh, that's Goldie. She wants to come in." So I opened the door, the cat walks in and Rene said, "You mean to tell me that cat knocks on the door to get in?" And I thought about that for a moment and said, "You know, that's exactly what she does!" and we collapsed into gales of laughter.

Professional pianist, composer, photographer, teacher and keyboard recording artist for over 40 years in New Orleans - until Katrina. Visit our website at: **http://fineimagesunlimited.blogspot.com** featuring the award winning notecard/pictures of photographer, Fritz Owens, and **http://www.owensstudios.com** for more information on his musical career.

"Cats always know whether people like or dislike them. They do not always care enough to do anything about it." ~ *Winifred Carriere*

Mi Gato es Ciego

By R.J. Peters

Anyone who can read Spanish knows that means "my cat is blind." For me, it also means that's her name.

When I began rescuing cats ten years ago, I had no idea how bad things were for so many of them. I naively thought I would be picking up healthy, friendly strays and finding them new homes right away. However, it was more like uncovering a secret underworld where animals of all species are treated badly in unimaginable scenarios of vicious cruelty, and people living "normal" lives never hear about it. In fact, it's so difficult to imagine what goes on, many people even refuse to believe it. I hadn't finished my first year of rescuing when I was rudely introduced to the shocking truth of animal cruelty and could hardly believe it myself. How could anyone...well, you know.

Since I had started the first cat rescue shelter in our area, there appeared to be a huge, collective sigh of relief as a flood of calls for help became an almost daily occurrence, overwhelming me, my resources, my helpers and my emotions. Until now, only a few dogs were being saved now and then. But no one gave much thought to the cats.

While cruelty is more common in some neighborhoods, people in cities and towns seem to know about it, to some degree, and have even come to accept it as a reality they can't control. However, there is a "dirty little secret" happening on some farms, where remoteness affords privacy, and unless someone calls it in, most of those abusive situations are never discovered. The general myth is that cats on farms are living a bucolic, comfortable life chasing birds and mice in the fields, with a cozy barn to nestle in at night. That may happen once in a while, but it's far from the greater reality of the difficult life they more commonly endure.

Fortunately for Ciego, someone cared and called me. All the cats on that farm were being systematically tortured and killed. Unfortunately, I was only able to get five kittens out of there. And only one of them survived, the one I later named Ciego. The other four perished over the next few days as their injuries were beyond help. Even Ciego's fate would not be clear for many weeks as she and I struggled to deal with her suffering. I didn't even know her eyes were gone at first, because her head was literally a ball of pus. Even her ears were plastered down in it and I feared they may have been cut off, like the kitten I had found inside a wall at a laundromat earlier.

I was relieved to see normal ears after a thorough and gentle cleaning, but I was heartbroken to discover her eyes were gone. Three veterinarians and everyone in our shelter group "suggested" she be euthanized. And I said no. We had decided to be a no-kill shelter and by golly, Ciego would not be killed on my watch. As long as there was breath in her body, I vowed to respect that and support it. However, if her prospects to survive diminished, I would choose euthanasia over suffering.

Since she was not welcome at the shelter, I took her home as my cat and treated her myself. There was nothing to lose but the battle, but it was one I was willing to fight. It took about 5 months of high dose antibiotics and almost constant personal attention to her physical needs, but she made it.

She is ten years old now and has permanent respiratory damage, but her spirit is completely healed. She loves everyone and is always the first to run to the door to greet anyone who comes over. She even begs strangers for hugs and petting by reaching up as high as she can against their legs, reaching out with one paw as if to shake hands.

She is an amazingly happy cat with a great personality and those who know her always ask about her first. She still loves to play, but as always, I have to limit her sessions to just a few minutes or she goes into respiratory distress, gasping for air and wheezing. Even when things are calm, she has a little "rattle" in her breathing. But she purrs a lot, and very loudly. I made a short video of her purring as she sat on my lap and have put it on my blog on the Internet: **http://loveablecat.blogspot.com/2011/07/ciego-purring-blind-kitty.html**

She has no trouble getting around in the house, but I decided some time ago it was time to quit my old habit of rearranging the furniture every few months. Dust bunnies accumulate more often now, but more importantly, Ciego always knows where she is.

>^..^<

"A cat has absolute emotional honesty: human beings, for one reason or another, may hide their feelings, but a cat does not."

~ Ernest Hemingway

Never Give Up Hope

By R.J. Peters

I was in the process of rescuing an abused dog when I spotted a small pet carrier off to one side. A small black cat was inside, for who knows how long, lying motionless on its side. So, as I led the dog away, I reached down and grabbed the carrier, too.

Once inside my van, I noticed the cat was not only alive but snuggled quietly against her were five tiny kittens - probably birthed right there in that tiny prison.

The dog had been through daily hell, according to neighbors' reports, but appeared to be in fairly good condition considering the frequent beatings he had endured for the past year.

He was treated by our veterinarian, cleaned up, and then later adopted to a loving older couple who gave him the home he deserved in the first place.

However, the cats were dehydrated and starving and required immediate emergency attention. The mother was very small, probably even too young to be birthing kittens already, and they didn't look like they would be around long, no matter what care they received. All the kittens were variously deformed and much too small, possibly born prematurely.

Somehow, though, one continued to hang on to life while the other four succumbed one by one over the next few days. She was totally black, like her mother, but had a corkscrew tail and short, misshapen legs on a very round body with a rat-like head. She was not cute. Yet I admired her tenacity and will to live and promised her and her mother I would do all I could to help them.

I named the devoted little queen Tara and her now only-kitten ended up with the nickname, Stubby. No one at the shelter expected her to live much longer, so little thought was given to a "real" name. Indeed, Stubby's entire first year was up for grabs as she continually had little setbacks – respiratory infections, eye infections, digestive problems – but we always conquered them and Stubby would be fine for a few more weeks.

In order to care for her most consistently and to be able to monitor her more frequently, I took her home. And yes, Tara came with her. They both flourished with regular care and the opportunity to bond with a family, and the uncertainty of Stubby's future faded from urgent concern to routine watchfulness. That is, until the seizures began.

The first one was slight and not definitive. It could have been the twitchings of a dream, where animals "run in place" as they sleep, chasing a fantasy toy or mouse.

But Stubby's "dreams" became more frequent and soon could not be dismissed as insignificant. I made an appointment with the vet, but when we got there, the senior vet was not in. His assistant, a brand new graduate, was taking patients that afternoon. As I explained what was happening and described Stubby's history, she had a seizure right there on the exam table. The vet freaked out. She had never seen this before and didn't know what to do. As she wrung her hands and cast about for inspiration, I asked if she advised euthanasia. After all, I didn't want Stubby to suffer. And if this vet couldn't figure out what was causing the convulsions and stop them, there was no time to find another vet now.

She vacillated and kept saying, "I don't know, I don't know..."

I grew impatient and simply took Stubby and left, saying, "Fine, I'll take her somewhere else." Only trouble was, there really was nowhere else to go in one day. It was already late afternoon, and vets in this rural area are typically up to 100 miles apart. So I did the only thing I could, really - I took her back home. I put her into a cage and gave her a "kitty tranquilizer" I had on hand for another cat in hopes she could relax and perhaps sleep. She was having 3 seizures an hour by then and needed some relief.

Well, she slept, all right. I thought she was dead! Exhausted with grief and worry and the day's long drive, I was too tired to dispose of her little body that night, so I left her in the cage overnight with plans to bury her the next day. But the next morning, when I went to the garage to get her, I was completely surprised by what I saw.

There was Stubby, sitting up and looking around. When she saw me, she started asking for food and reaching through the bars of the cage door. I couldn't run to the kitchen fast enough to make her some breakfast, and she couldn't eat it fast enough when I slipped her dish into the cage. I stood there in awe, watching her eat. She even purred as she consumed the raw chicken I happened to have in the refrigerator for the other cats who were being raw fed. And that was the day Stubby became one of the "strict carnivores" in our house, eating only raw meat.

She recovered swiftly, and amazingly never had another seizure. I took her to another vet to be sure she was healthy, and her story was one the vet had never heard before. In fact, if I had gone there first, Stubby would have been euthanized. So, while I was annoyed with the indecisiveness of the new vet in another town, I also was very grateful that she didn't know what to do.

Stubby is now nine years old and still eats raw meat as her primary diet. She might even be the healthiest cat we have!

She remains very small and is difficult to photograph...you know how some people just don't "take a good picture?" Well, Stubby is like that. But she doesn't care, so neither do we. She's one of our miracle kitties and we hope she has at least nine more years!

>^..^<

"The smallest feline is a masterpiece." ~ *Leonardo Da Vinci*

The Cat Husband, "Karlos A. Kitty"

By A.L. Wilson

It was the spring of 2001 in Phoenix, Arizona (just before the events of "9/11"), and I chose that year to attempt to lose some of the 60 plus pounds I gained in my late marriage. I joined a diet clinic that administered massive B vitamin shots and had an eating plan laid out to coincide. I was in the tiny strip mall in Glendale, Arizona and as I exited my vehicle, I was approached by an all grey cat speaking to me excitedly.

The small shopping center was surrounded by apartments and I assumed he must belong to someone living close by. I talked to the nervous kitty and petted him briefly, then went into the clinic for my shot and weigh in. I asked after him in the office and the receptionist indicated he had been out there 2 days in a row and was approaching anyone and everyone.

This changed things a bit since it was obvious he was lost and had not been found by whoever owned him. He did not appear disheveled, dirty, nor did he seem to have suffered any injury thus far. He was probably getting very hungry and thirsty and unless someone made the effort to help him get home it was looking as though he would not get there by himself and would eventually starve, get hit by a car or something worse. He was well cared for, sporting thick clean fur, and he was declawed and neutered. I found it hard to believe that with 2 days gone no one had come looking for him as everything else spoke of loved pet.

I inspected him further and found he was complaining due to his front paw being covered in hardening tar. He would have a time of it running, climbing and defending himself should the need arise. I decided to take him home and post some flyers in the area with my number so he could go home if anyone took the time to look. I figured a quick trip to the vet to remove the tar would be an opportunity to check for a microchip should he have one.

I set about looking for a box to contain him for the trip as you never can tell how a cat will react to a ride in a car. There were few shops in the mall and no boxes. I heard suggestions from some about placing the cat in the trunk (unthinkable!) and one woman volunteered a blanket that was dirtier than this cat would ever hope to be. I figured I would go home and return with a carrier. He had been hanging around for 2 days so it was safe to figure he would be there for a few hours more. I stooped down and looked into his eyes and explained that I would be right back and that we would get his paw cleaned up and a meal in him, not to worry, and to just wait here until I returned.

I guess he wasn't taking any chances with the only human who had stopped to pay any attention and he was not about to miss the one opportunity that had come to him to get out of this scary situation. He walked behind me and as I opened my car door he slipped inside and seated himself politely in the passenger side sitting upright and staring out the windshield waiting for us to pull out. I was about to hustle him out worrying that my plush velour upholstery would be ruined when I thought better of it. He looked so well behaved and had placed himself in the car with no coaching whatsoever. He must certainly know what happens in a car... he was obviously familiar with seating arrangements.

I got in, started up the vehicle, and looked over to see if his composure had fled. He continued to sit bolt upright and would occasionally glance over at me to let me know he was assessing my driving skills. I drove in disbelief at this cat's almost human-like demeanor. At one point, due to the distraction, I was forced to slam on my brakes or rear-end someone in front of me. The short stop wasn't too severe but he slid onto the floor with an ungainly thump and once recovered and in his seat again, gave me a cautioning look that said I had best pay better attention to where we were going or he would have to summon another ride; this mistake was not to happen again. He got up on his hind legs at every stop the rest of the trip, placing his feet on the dash. He craned his neck around, doing a double check on the traffic and our general position (just to make sure). I carried him with no resistance once we arrived at the vet and placed him in the receptionist's arms. He watched me over her shoulder as they disappeared down the hall to be bathed and checked for an identifying microchip.

The receptionist was also my roommate at the time so I picked them both up at 5pm expecting to hear that she had found a chip in him and had spoken with his owner.

Surprisingly, he had no chip. He was, as it turned out, a very sweet natured kitty. My vet placed his age around 5 to 6 years old. He settled in immediately, sleeping on her chest, stretched full length, every toe extended, a satisfied look on his peaceful little cat face.

She insisted that she wanted to keep this cat and since I had recently taken on 3 more kittens that were abandoned and had health issues, I saw no reason to protest her wanting him.

As is always the case, at least in my experience, roommates on the whole are hardly worth the effort even if you are sleeping with them and then barely at that. It was with little surprise that the friendly relationship was quick to sour between us and since it was my apartment, she was going to be the one to leave. During her day at work shortly thereafter, I packed her up, and when she returned from work, found her belongings all neatly packed and labeled outside the backdoor with a letter explaining that since she had ignored my requests to find other accommodations I was helping things along. She made her request that I place her cat in a carrier outside with her belongings at an exact time when she would return for her things. The request failed to include this sweet grey cat she had supposedly wanted for her own so badly.

In return, I failed to ask if she wanted to take him along with her other kitty.

She had named him for a character out of a TV show called "Walker Texas Ranger." One of the rangers in the show was a good looking Hispanic guy named "Carlos."

The grey cat hardly looked the part of being either Hispanic or a "Texas Ranger" but he had learned his name and changing it would have been difficult, so "Carlos" it was. I figured the least I could do was spell it with a "K" like the German "Karl" and being fond of playing with words it developed into a full name complete with middle initial and last name.

He was now "Karlos A. Kitty" and he would live with me for 10 years almost to the day and be special in a way I have never known before or since, at least regarding relationships with cats.

Karlos quickly showed himself to be a special soul. He showed qualities not usual in the average house cat. He was quiet and acquiesced quickly to all the other cats in the household. He staked no territory and was meek to a fault. I found myself defending him as he would not defend himself against any other cat. He would back away, look down, and hang his head slightly and slowly walk away from any confrontation. He didn't cower nor was he a nervous animal. He simply didn't want to be involved in anything aggressive whatsoever. When new kittens arrived, he would watch over them like a nanny or governess their first week or so in the home. He would sleep with them, walk them to the bowls to eat and sit by, watching that they ate unmolested and made sure they knew where the cat box was and that they paid a regular visit to the area just to make sure they got the idea and had ample opportunity to develop the preferred habits. If they got themselves stuck somewhere that he couldn't coach them out of, he came to me and herded me to the place they were in and sat by while I extricated them from whatever spot they were in.

All this and he never made a sound. No meow, no trill, no ackackack chortling. Since the first day when he spoke to me quite loudly and directly, not a sound. Not even the mouth open with no sound coming out (the silent meow), not even that attempt.

We moved to a bigger apartment. The morning of the 911 New York trade towers incident I was making a pot of coffee for myself and friend when he strutted into the kitchen and without a moment's hesitation jumped straight up into my arms and clung to my neck with his forearms, head-butting me fiercely and nuzzling me hard.

I tried to put him down once and he wasn't even all the way on the floor when he jumped right back up. I settled for walking around with him clinging to me the rest of the morning. I was watching a movie when my ex-husband called, really upset. So much so he wasn't making any sense... just something about what have they done to NY. He was a native of New York and had grown up in the Bronx. I flipped channels back into the TV and out of the VCR to find every channel covering the plane crash on the towers with the smoke and devastation replaying.

The nation was in shock and horror at the incident, and it wasn't right away, but I noticed after a bit that Karlos was no longer hanging from my neck but sitting nearby and watching me.

Karlos was never aggressive, nor was he social. He did not participate in "cat" politics around the home; he just wanted to be by me and know where I was. He slept at the head of the bed on my pillow. If I was ill and in bed after all the rest had paid their respects and gone off to play, he would remain lying next to me, moving when I moved or readjusting only after a trip to the bowl or box.

Years went by and in the winter he took to sleeping under the covers with me. He would wait until we all settled in and then come up and head butt me so I would know to lift the covers up so he could climb under. He would turn around and then lie down with his head in the crook of my arm facing me and stretch his little arm out and curve it around my neck, pulling us close together. His nose would touch mine and he would dip his head down slightly. A little nest, just Karlos and me, warm and safe together under the covers. My husband said he was close to me in a special way like my child and my husband all in one. That he was grateful I had rescued him, he called him my cat husband.

In 2006 I had a hip replaced and had a bad drug reaction after surgery, which landed me in a coma for 24 hrs. On my return home he wouldn't leave my side except to hit the box and eat and drink. My recovery was several months and he attended me the entire time.

When I went back to work, he knew down to the minute just about when I should be home and would pester my husband if I was late. He had a signature move he would make with me. He would take his paw which was small and round and place it

64

directly over the tip of my nose, the little fingertip pads across the top of my nose, the bigger pad of the palm area below.

Without ever realizing it, I had come to depend on this sweet little creature's love and affection. His spot in my world was highlighted when on occasion he went wandering.

We keep indoor cats and do not allow our cats to go out unattended. Karlos was a bit sneaky at times and would wait near the door hidden from view. When the door would open, he would jet out quickly, hiding in the closest shrubbery, and then when you were gone out of sight, he would come out and meander a bit. He liked to watch the birds and chase them, though he never caught a single one his entire life. He wasn't the great hunter but he liked to frolic after them.

On finding himself tired of the game he would look up to find he was lost. Not a clue where he was or how to get home, he was smart enough to know he would only make it worse trying to get home on his own and learned that we would be out to find him if he did not return within a certain amount of time. He would at times not go far and when bored of the game return to the door and speak once like a magician, to gain entrance. Oddly, as close as we were and as much as I fretted when he had gone on one of his little trips, it was always my husband's keen ear that would catch the single sound Karlos made and go to let him in. Even when I listened and strained to hear it.

Once he was gone an extraordinarily long time as he had managed to take off shortly after dinner. The next day after 1 o'clock when he failed to return, I sent my poor husband to walk the residential streets of our neighborhood in over 100 degree heat searching for my Karlos. It took a long time, but finally Dan came back carrying Karlos, hot, dirty and completely unashamed of how he had worried me.

In the spring of 2010 I was laid off due to the economic crisis in the U.S. During my first week home I noticed that Karlos had lost weight, enough to concern me. I had been working over 40 hours and often came home only to eat dinner and slump into bed exhausted. I looked more closely and, horrified, I realized he was emaciated. He had been for a surgery on his ear 4 months prior for a hematoma and once home had seemed a bit depressed, but I figured it was just the trauma of the vet trip, anesthesia, and overnight stay apart from me and that it would dissipate shortly.

I took to feeding him special food on the advice from a pet naturopath. I switched him to raw meat. He seemed to get tired of eating and quit, so it took quite a bit of coaxing on my part. He had a sore on his tail that would not heal and he had developed a bad smell to his fur. I loved him so dearly I never let it bother me but tucked him in and held him just as close. He gained a little weight back and the smell cleared some, but the sore would not heal, and further it would bleed if not kept bandaged. I hated myself; once a wage earner that would take an animal to the vet for the slightest wheeze, I was now having a hard time feeding them all. People told me I should take them to the humane society. I tried to be optimistic and kept looking for work. Seven months went by. No work, and Karlos was not getting better. Our car laid down dead in the carport; both my husband and I were unemployed. My husband collapsed on the floor of our living room one morning and was rushed to the hospital for an emergency procedure.

That night I asked my neighbor to help me change Karlos' bandage since she had a couple cats and would know how to aid me. After I was done, she looked at me and told me she wanted to pay to have him taken to the vet. She said she had the money and she wanted to do this. I was relieved and the next day we went to see the vet in our neighborhood. I was ashamed when I placed my poor friend on the table he was so thin. He had hung in for a long time dutifully sleeping with me and allowing me to minister to him every way I could. I knew this would be a big expense, but I figured no matter what, I would find a way to pay for it now that we were in the door. It never crossed my mind that he would not come home with me that day.

Dr. Babcock was very kind and explained that Karlos had a cancer on his tail and that if it had not spread to the rest of his body, it would be amputated and he would recover with intensive nursing care on my part, but if it had spread to the rest of the body, that wouldn't be an option.

We did a full body x-ray and when they came back and placed him in my arms, I knew. The cancer was throughout his body and he was now in pain. I would have to put him to sleep as he was suffering and hanging on just for me. No decision, no matter how clear-cut and obvious, has ever tortured me more. They left us alone for awhile and I told him how much I loved him and that I was sorry but I did not want to be selfish anymore, that I would see him as soon as I could.

They placed him on a pretty blanket with flowers and the doctor gave him a small injection while I held him. He relaxed against my arm and then I felt the body become empty.

I have cried every day since he left. Two years later I still cry but I hide it from friends and family. I avoid going to bed at night because there is no Karlos to come to bed with me anymore. I thought at first that maybe I could get another kitty like him and that we would become close and I would not hurt so badly. I went to shelters, cat shows, and scoured the Internet.

I felt almost desperate to relieve the aching emptiness. Finally I faced the truth: there is no other cat like my Karlos. I was lucky I have known the joy of a cat husband...and now I am a kitty widow. I make sure I take the time to know all my cats individually and I love them each and every one. I make sure they each know they are special to me. I miss Karlos and that won't change. I don't talk about it, but it is an empty burning pain, so I avoid the sore spot. When I leave this body and this world, I will know if I am in heaven or in hell, as I will just look around for Karlos. It isn't heaven if my kitty husband isn't there. In the meantime, I try to be good because I know Karlos is in heaven and I don't want to disappoint him.

A cat that made me want to be a better person, he was that kind, loving, and precious. That little grey kitty I found in a parking lot was that close to me. That is a very special kitty in my book.

>^..^<

A.J. Wilson works for a delivery service in Phoenix, Arizona doing tech support and administrative duties. She has been rescuing and raising cats for 30 years in both the California Bay Area and Phoenix. She and her husband currently share their lives with 7 amazing kitties.

"You can tell your cat anything and he'll still love you. If you lose your job or your best friend, your cat will think no less of you."

~ Helen Powers

A Yellow Tabby Named Kitty

By Dena Johannes

For all of my childhood and much of my adulthood I have always been a dog lover and never even considered the companionship of a furry feline, simply because I was terrified of their sharp claws and also believed that cats were just not personable animals. I believed through my own ignorance that cats were a one-person animal and they could not show you the affection that dogs could because they seemed to me to just meander around and provide no distinctive traits that appealed to me.

I am four years from 60 and have had my eyes opened to the world of felines, first through my granddaughters who had a yellow tabby cat they named Kitty. I was never one to go up and pet a cat or really have an interest, like I said, because I was terrified of their claws. I do not know where that fear came from because I don't remember having any kind of a bad experience with a cat or its claws as a young child. All I knew was when a cat came near me my instinct said to avoid the furry little critters.

My opinion of cats started to slowly change when I would watch my granddaughters interact with their cat they called Kitty. One of the most amazing and funniest things I ever watched was when my granddaughters would play with their cat as if she were a doll. I will never forget the times of laughing so hard that tears would stream down my face when Kitty was dressed in doll clothes, a baby bonnet, and to top it off, pink lipstick. Do not ask me how they accomplished it, but it was truly one of the funniest things I had ever witnessed.

As time passed, I grew to understand how the lipstick was plausible! Kitty was not only a cat but also a cat that truly took on the personality of a human. Kitty liked to be dressed up in doll clothes, didn't seem to mind lipstick, enjoyed stroller rides and was not afraid of water, as in bath water! This cat knew comfort and it did not include the floor, or a cat bed. Kitty's favorite place to sleep was on a pillow on my granddaughter's bed. If you could not find her, it was a sure bet if you pulled the covers back that is where she would be. I was also told that cats hated water; not this one!

When my daughter and granddaughters were getting ready to move, they found out that the area where they were going to live did not allow animals, and it was a strict ordinance that was adhered to. My granddaughters were heart broken to think that Kitty would have to go to a new home. That is where I came in, the new home for Kitty. I would have to say, I never hesitated when my granddaughters asked if I would give her a home because I had grown to really like her over time.

As time passed and Kitty became familiar with her new surroundings, we formed a special bond that freed me from the fear of something as silly as cat claws! When I was home, she followed me around just like a dog will do, and when I sat down, many times she wanted to be in my lap for attention. I found a new love for an animal that I never dreamed I could ever get close to. I broadened my horizon and found out that a cat can be as lovable as a dog and like anything else you can't always believe what you hear when it comes to anyone else's opinions about any animal. I believe that most creatures, if treated properly with love and affection, can reciprocate by showing you through their own behavior how they feel about you!

As my short story ends so does the whereabouts of a cat that I had grown to love and care about over time. On a day of one of her outdoor excursions, she failed to come home as she did everyday before that. I searched for days on end, and called neighbors but she was never found. The only conclusion that I could reach was that someone else saw what I did in her and decided to give her a home. Sad but true that an animal can have so much character that someone else will claim them and leave you heartbroken!

>^..^<

Dena Johannes is a late-blooming cat lover, devoted to family, friends and her pets.

"Don't let anyone tell you loving a cat is silly. Love, in any form, is a precious commodity." ~ Barbara L. Diamond

Cats May Really Have 9 Lives – My Miracle Cat

By Cheryl Wright

I know we all joke about cats having 9 lives, but in a way, I feel like my cat, Gus, really did. Let me explain...

My mother brought Gus to me in 1997. She had found him as a stray kitty and had taken him home. However, I had just lost a kitty, and since she already had a number of cats, we agreed that Gus would be welcome in my home.

In 2005, we noticed that Gus seemed to be drinking a lot of water and having what seemed to be an excess amount of urine. He also began spraying the walls. I discussed this with my mother, who has a lot of experience with cats. She thought he may have diabetes and suggested I definitely take him to the vet, which I did.

Sure enough, Gus was diagnosed with diabetes. His blood sugar level was in the low 500s (normal is around 150). Wow! I had never heard of a cat having diabetes. So, we started him on a special, high-protein diet, and we began giving him insulin.

We first started with 1.5 units of insulin twice a day, and kept checking his blood sugar level every two weeks. I would take him to the vet and leave him there all day, so they could do an insulin curve (basically they would check his sugar level 3 times during the day). We had to increase the amount of insulin to 2, then 2.5, then 3, then 3.5, then 4 units, twice a day.

One day, after a few months, I found Gus lying in the closet, one of his favorite places to lie... only this time something didn't seem right. He had peed on the bed and pooped on the floor, and didn't seem like he had much energy. I called the emergency vet to see if there was something I could give him for sugar, but they suggested I just bring him in.

As it turns out, his blood sugar had dropped to 28. The vet said she was amazed he was still alert at all. They gave him a sugar boost to bring his blood sugar back up, and then told me that if I hadn't brought him in, he would have died. (Here I think Gus used up at least one of his lives.) I took him home after a couple of hours, and we dropped his insulin dose to 1 unit twice a day. I also bought some Karo syrup to keep on hand for any possible future emergency.

Then we went through the same scenario described above, monitoring him every two weeks and increasing the insulin each time. We ultimately reached a level of 3 units, twice a day.

Then, after another few months, I had to attend a weekend seminar. I had requested that my husband give Gus his shots. My husband hadn't, up to this point, given him any shots, and wasn't really comfortable doing it. However, he agreed to do it so I could go the seminar. I asked him if he knew how to do it, and he said, "Yes." I didn't actually show him how to do it or how much to give (which was my mistake). I just told him to give 3 units twice a day.

He gave Gus a shot on Friday night and Saturday morning; he couldn't find Gus Saturday night, so he missed that shot; and then again on Sunday morning. When I came home on Sunday afternoon, I saw Gus in my bedroom, tangled up in some stereo wires, and he wasn't moving. There was poop everywhere. I screamed, "Oh my God! He's dead!" and I ran over to him. I noticed he was still breathing, but was otherwise completely unresponsive. I asked my husband how much insulin he had given him. It turns out that he had been giving him 30 units, not 3 units, which meant that Gus had received 90 units of insulin in just under two days. He was literally on death's doorstep at this point.

I immediately grabbed some Karo syrup and rubbed it on his gums, but I could tell that Gus was much too critical for that to help. I grabbed him in my arms and rushed to the emergency vet. I ran in with him yelling, "He needs sugar now! He's in insulin shock!" They immediately took him from me and started an IV with sugar.

They said they would keep him overnight, continue the IV, and monitor him continuously. The next day, Monday, they told me he was responsive, but that there was still so much insulin in him they needed to keep him yet another day. I went to the vet to visit with him and see how he was doing, but agreed to let them keep him until he was out of danger.

They had to give him sugar boosts a couple of times along with the IV, but eventually, his sugar level started to come back within his normal range. Finally, during the night, they started weaning him from the IV, and his sugar actually went back high again. They were supposed to release him to me Tuesday morning at 9am, but then I got a call from the vet. They told me they thought he went blind.

Normally, Gus would hiss and spit at anyone trying to get him in or out of his cage. But Tuesday morning, he didn't do anything.

They started trying to verify if he could or couldn't see. They determined that he couldn't see. The doctor said it was possible that his brain had swollen from the dramatic sugar level changes and it could be pressing on the skull, thus creating the blindness. It could go away, or it could be permanent damage, which can happen with diabetics.

They suggested that they keep him yet another day (and another $600) so they could give him a medicine to reduce the possible brain swelling and see if this made a difference. I discussed this with my mother again, and her suggestion was simply to bring him home. He had already been through so much. Besides, cats can still live happy lives being blind. I also discussed this with my regular vet, who suggested that I simply visit with him first and then decide what I wanted to do.

I went to see Gus. He seemed like he was doing okay, other than not being able to see. He welcomed the love and attention, but I could tell he was certainly tired of being there. I decided to bring him home, so he could be in a comfortable environment, and we could give him love and attention. If he was blind, then, so be it.

We brought him home and took him to the bedroom where he liked to be most of the time. He wandered around a bit, smelling things and occasionally bumping into things. I put him on the bed, and he cautiously jumped back down. He eventually began wandering through the entire house. He found all the essentials – litter box, food, and water. We even let him outside in the backyard, and he liked just hanging out in the grass. He was certainly more docile as a blind cat, and he seemed like he would get by just fine.

For the next few days, we kept testing him to see if perhaps his eyesight would return. We would wave our hands in front of his face, stick our hands out to see if he would come over, throw cotton balls at him, etc. It went on like this for about 4 days. Then, one day I noticed him "watching" me. I walked across the room and he seemed to follow my movements. So we threw a Q-tip on the floor, which he then began playing with. I thought, "There's no way he could do that if he couldn't see." So, we just kept watching and testing him. More and more I was becoming convinced that he could, in fact, see again.

Finally, one day Gus was outside and my husband turned on the sprinklers. He didn't see Gus in the yard. Gus darted out of the grass and straight through the cat door to the house so fast it was shocking! It was then that I was absolutely convinced he could see again. We were so happy and relieved to have Gus back – in full!

We did not put Gus back on insulin for a few months. After a while, though, I started noticing increased urine output, so I had his sugar level checked again. We did end up starting insulin again, but kept it to 1 unit twice daily. He did well on that regimen for a while. We took him to the vet periodically to do a fructose test for a snapshot of his blood sugar, and would adjust the insulin accordingly.

After a couple of years, we had yet a third incident where Gus just didn't seem quite "right" to me. So, I took him to the vet to have his sugar checked, and it was again down to 30. We took him off the insulin again, and for some reason, he seemed to not need it anymore. He never went back on the insulin after this. We could tell he was getting older, and may not live much longer, and we just wanted to enjoy our time with him.

Then, at a checkup, the vet told me that all of Gus's teeth had rotted, and that he must be in terrible pain. We tried putting antibiotics directly on his gums, but he just wouldn't tolerate that. I switched him to a canned/wet food diet only, which was still a high-protein, diabetic cat food.

My vet suggested that we consider euthanizing him due to how much pain she assumed he must be in. The thought of putting him to sleep broke my heart, and yet I didn't want him to suffer. So, I decided to have a mobile vet come do it at our home. If I had to euthanize him, I wanted him to be at home and as comfortable as possible.

When the mobile vet examined him, she disagreed with my primary vet. She thought he didn't seem like he was in terrible pain (not to say he was pain-free), and that he just didn't seem "ready" to go. So, we started him on a few natural treatments as well as another type of antibiotic. After a while, I finally just stopped trying to give him anything, so as to not "torture" him anymore. I wanted to just love him and make him as comfortable as possible. He lived for a full year more.

Eventually it was his time to go. He was probably somewhere around 18 or 19 years old. He had lived with diabetes for the last six or seven years of his life. He had some major trials, and eventually used up his nine lives. He was a wonderful kitty, and I will forever miss him. Now I just picture him living on the other side of the Rainbow Bridge with no more sickness and a full set of healthy teeth.

>^..^<

Cheryl L. Wright is a certified Life Coach having received certification in 2010 from Southwest Institute of Healing Arts. She also acquired certification in Massage Therapy in 1999 from New Mexico School of Natural Therapeutics, and is currently studying Holistic Nutrition. She holds a Bachelor of Arts Degree in Electronics Engineering Technology from DeVry Institute of Technology and has maintained a successful career in technology for 23 years. Currently living in Arizona with her husband, two children, a dog, a cat, and two fish, she has had pets her entire life.

"No amount of time can erase the memory of a good cat, and no amount of masking tape can ever totally remove his fur from your couch." ~ Leo Dworken

Bumper

By Cheryl Wright

Bumper was born under the headboard of my bed. His mama was a Siamese kitty, named Precious, and this was her second litter. I hadn't kept any from the first litter, but really wanted to keep one from her second, and last, litter, since I had her spayed after that. She gave birth to six kittens during the night in the little tiny space available underneath the headboard of my waterbed. There were three orange tabbies and three black and white kittens.

They were, of course, simply adorable. Bumper was one of the black and white kittens and was the fluffiest of all of them.

We didn't actually name him Bumper right off the bat. We had tried many different names for him, but nothing had really stuck yet. When he was just a couple months old, and the only kitten left at home, he, like so many kittens, had tons of energy. He would repeatedly tear through the house as fast as he could. On several occasions, he was running and didn't stop until he hit the slick linoleum bathroom floor, which, of course, then he couldn't stop. He hit the linoleum and then slid head first into the side of the bathtub.

Thump! Then he would sit there and shake his head. I felt bad for him, and yet it was so funny. My roommate at the time started calling him "Bump Head." I didn't like that name and shortened it to Bumper. That name stuck.

Bumper was a great kitty, and as a responsible pet owner, I had him neutered at six months of age. He, Precious and Slick (my third kitty) all hung out together, and we had a great time. Bumper was very friendly, playful AND affectionate.

When Bumper was about 1 ½ years old, I was in college at the time, and I needed to move to another location. I had left my beloved kitties in the care of someone I thought was responsible, during my transition. That turned out to be a big mistake. He locked them all outside, and they all three disappeared. I was crushed. I called animal control, the Humane Society, and every shelter I could find to report my missing kitties hoping that they would be found and turned in. I placed notices around the neighborhood. Several weeks passed and no word. I kept calling. Nothing.

Then, one day, I got a call from the Humane Society. They had a cat that resembled the description of one of mine. I immediately drove over there. It was Bumper! He had been there for four days already, and had been placed up for adoption. Yes, that quickly! I actually saw a couple looking at him. I yelled, "That's my cat! That's my cat!" and ran over to the cage where he was. He recognized me and starting mewing for me to get him. The couple that had been looking at him stepped aside, and indicated they were very happy for us to have found each other again. I opened the cage, and Bumper willing let me scoop him up and hold him tight. I had to pay the adoption fee, since they had already examined him and placed him there. I think it was about $30 at the time. That was a lot of money for me, but I wouldn't consider not paying it to have my beloved Bumper back! Sadly, I never saw Precious or Slick again. But I was grateful to at least have Bumper.

Shortly after that, I graduated from college and moved to another state, of course, taking Bumper with me. Bumper had so many good qualities. He was "the life of the party" anytime I had visitors. Most cats run and hide when visitors come, but not Bumper. He wanted to be right in the middle of it all. And if anyone got up out of their seat, Bumper was quick to jump up and take their spot. All my friends just adored him.

He was also very cuddly. He loved to sleep with me. He would lay on his side, facing me, with his head on the pillow. Then he would stretch out his front leg and rest his paw on my neck. It was like he was hugging me every night. I loved cuddling with Bumper. And when I started dating, Bumper seemed a bit jealous. If, at any time, I had an overnight guest, Bumper would ensure that he snuggled up very close to me, in between me and my partner. Bumper would not let anyone else be next to me. I didn't mind. Bumper and I had been through a lot together.

Bumper lived to be just nine years old. Sadly, he got sick very suddenly. We suspected he may have gotten into some antifreeze or something. He seemed fine one day, and the next, he was in obvious pain. I rushed him to the vet, and upon examination, they determined that his kidneys were failing. His creatinine level was eleven, when a normal level is around two. We put Bumper on an IV for two days to see if we could flush out the kidneys. Unfortunately, that didn't help, and he continued to worsen. His creatinine level rose to sixteen. We knew he was suffering, and had to make the very difficult decision to end his suffering. Since he already had an IV, it made the process a bit easier. I held him in my lap and loved him while the doctor added the necessary chemicals to the IV. Bumper was purring, then his head got heavy and he went to sleep, never to wake again. I cried as I held him and was so sad to say good-bye, and yet I was so grateful for the time I had with him. He was my best cat ever.

>^..^<

"Another cat? Perhaps. For love there is also a season; its seeds must be resown. But a family cat is not replaceable like a wornout coat or a set of tires. Each new kitten becomes its own cat, and none is repeated. I am four cats old, measuring out my life in friends that have succeeded but not replaced one another."
- Irving Townsend

The Cat That Shopped For a New Home
- Special Lessons from a Stray Cat

By Cateline Beem

I'd seen this gorgeous feline around before. For a couple years I believe. It would come into the back garden, look around, and then mosey on back from whence it came. It never stayed long... at least as I could see.

I suspected it might be one of the special charges a neighbor was harboring out of the goodness of her heart. It looked well fed...but was definitely browsing the neighborhood. And that is not a good thing usually. In this neighborhood, with a couple of known cat haters, all the more worrisome.

I chatted with this charitable neighbor one day, while frantically trying to locate a lost boy of mine who escaped. He was a silver tabby with just incredible, perfect markings, making him look regal and ever-gorgeous.

I had posted a picture of him in the neighborhood, but it had to be enlarged from a tiny polaroid and wasn't the best...but all I had. My neighbor contacted me and asked me about my lost baby...and said that there was a really uniquely marked cat that had been staying with her. After she described it, I knew it wasn't my special boy, but suspected it was the lovely feline that had been paying visits to our back garden.

Months passed, and suddenly, as the weather grew colder, that same wonderfully beautiful cat was now showing up more frequently and now coming onto our back porch. I was able to talk softly to it, and although wary and not approachable, it would linger and listen and watch. Then it would be gone.

After a while, as the winter approached more rapidly, this gorgeous feline took to settling for a snooze on the back porch. I had an insulated dog/cat house out there for my cats to use when allowed some supervised outdoor action, and it was available to any poor lost or abandoned life that needed protection from the cold, the dangers of the street and some humans.

I put out some food to see if it might be hungry...and of course some fresh water. It is always such a risk for cats in colder weather, when people add anti-freeze to their cars. Cats can easily be attracted to the fatal liquid, especially if thirsty, and lap it up. And if you have ever been witness to an animal dying of anti-freeze poisoning...you'll *never ever* forget it. It is ample content for many, many nights of nasty nightmares. Heartbreaking, terribly painful and torturous to witness and a horrific way to die. I speak from experience. And it was suspected that one of our human neighbors was deliberately setting out this inhumanely cruel death trap.

Our lovely visitor approached with much caution after I retreated inside and hungrily devoured the soft canned food I'd provided. I always like to add some vitamins for my own cats, but especially for poor strays that may not get another meal or clean, wholesome food for a while, and who may already suffer from malnutrition along with other maladies and/or wounds.

I set out a cozy rug and towel bed covered by a wind blocker made from a clear blanket box. I retreated into the house. Our feline friend returned and settled in. But not IN the protective bedroom I'd created...but rather atop it! The 'house' that was already there likely carried too much scent from our own crew. It never went inside it.

The cold wind blew and rattled the windows. Yet our fuzzy friend remained out in the open, atop the box, snoozing away, so desperate to remain at the ready and determined to retain its freedom. It must have welcomed the morning sun to warm its bones.

As the days passed, more nutritious food, along with some warm water...' kitty tea' I call it... was placed outside daily. The cat watched me with great interest...and great caution. I always spoke to it...and created some special words that it would get used to hearing from me, in the hopes that it would eventually allow me to approach.

Weeks went by. Winter had settled in for long months of chill-to-and-through-the-bone and piles of snow, which was never welcome. We were in for a brutal season.

During this time, our cat visitor became a night-time resident. Where it spent the day, I'm not sure. Perhaps she went back to the neighbor's house. My neighbor had mentioned to me that the cat we'd chatted about previously, as I searched for my missing kitty boy, would not utilize her garage. She'd prepared a little shelter there for her and other homeless little hearts that she protected. She left the garage door open at the bottom...but this kitty would never go in. She stayed outdoors somewhere. So I knew that this lovely lady had decided to take up night residence, at least, with us. It may have become too crowded for her liking at her former residence. But it snowed, it rained, the wind and ice blew fiercely, and this feline remained atop the box, snow alighting atop her back... It mattered not. It stayed where it was. I've never seen a cat so tough to weather the storms - literally - in this way. It was worrisome actually, that she would not take shelter.

As each day went on...I ventured to reach out my finger to see if she would sniff it...in hopes of getting her to allow me to pet her at some point -- and eventually handle her. I wanted to get her some vet care. Although she looked great...just a big slender, slinky absolutely gorgeously marked silver tabby with cream and gold accents, you never know what might lurk inside. And I certainly wanted to arrange to have her neutered so that no additional lives would meet such unfortunate life struggles.

As time passed, and the peak of winter was approaching, I finally had success! My lovely outdoor resident allowed me to gently touch her forehead! But not more! Anything more was duly swatted away with a swift bat of her paw. And that's how I discovered that this solitary feline was also declawed. So this lass had definitely had a family at one time, yet must have experienced something very negative to be soooo wary of humans, so terrified of touch, so very aloof, solitary and intensely watchful.

Declawed. A very painful, usually unnecessary procedure that can create additional problems for a cat. For a poor feline out on its own, whether lost or discarded, this poses even more difficulties.

If the cat would need to hunt to survive, if it even knew how, it would be very difficult without front claws. Behavioral changes can also be noted in many cats without their natural defenses. They can become more nervous, irritable and defensive, and some of those I've harbored from the storms of life were more prone to spray or toilet inappropriately. And if it 'itches' where back claws can't reach, they endure even more. Some cats are even subjected to the removal of all four claws. Just imagine.

A cat without claws can only defend itself by up-close-and-personal-biting, which usually leads to severe and often life-threatening wounds and nasty feline diseases such as feline AIDS and feline leukemia. This is bound to alter behavior to a more nervous, defensive mode. If you can scare or ward off a potential aggressor, far better than to risk your life by having to get into face-to-face battle with one's teeth, thus exposing eyes, head, neck and other body areas to injuries that can become infected and/or be severe enough to lead to death. Not to mention the suffering, pain and hunger, which all grow worse as the cat becomes sicker, unable to find food or shelter while on this undeserved journey to demise. Flies often lay eggs in their wounds, leading to maggot infestation as well, which eat away the flesh, sometimes also entering the cat's anal canal, making things more serious and difficult for the poor creature.

Cats often seek to hide when they are sick or injured, trying to find comfort and protection from other attackers when weak. And if they cannot walk well or at all and also have no means to defend themselves other than a growl, they are open to dangers from other cats and even possibly humans. Cats out on their own often die an undeserved, lonely, painful death.

While these terrible diseases, FIV and FeLV, are not immediately fatal, they eventually lead to unhappy deaths, as the immune system is weakened and they are now more open to any number of afflictions that lead to death. Further, even though cats can live happily for years with either or both of these diseases, they are often the first to be put to death if captured and/or surrendered to some 'shelters,' who save their space for more healthy individuals, who also cite the difficulties in finding homes for animals with these conditions.

I have given permanent homes to more than a few cats with either - or both diseases together- and enjoyed their company for years. One must take some precautions to separate them from other healthy cats and arrange sometimes some special accommodation. But it is not an immediate death sentence, as these poor creatures are sometimes sadly given at some vets' offices and shelters. They can be susceptible to more afflictions along the way, but I have had great success enjoying the love and personalities of these sweet, unfortunate creatures for many years before their final days.

I soooo hoped that this lovely creature had somehow, despite her now very limited defenses, escaped this fate.

As each day passed, I made efforts to continue to gain my new girl's trust. She was just so lovely, so sleek, so sweet. She acted like a female, but was larger than I would have expected. So I couldn't be sure of her gender. She wouldn't allow me to get up close, or lift her tail long enough to decipher her heritage. But her overall demeanor seemed to register as a female -- and she became known to our household as "Salinka." It fit her so well.

Before spring was visible around the bend, Salinka now was allowing me to pet her head, and very much enjoyed it. And then eventually, I was allowed to stroke her very gently down her back. I started to gently scratch her ears, rub her neck...but was always held in check by her swift swat and loud vocals when she'd had enough of my affections.

To my surprise, one morning as I opened the door to deliver her breakfast, she jumped down off the box and decided to come right into the house!

She immediately looked around, noticed the other cats - which I'm sure she knew about - - and sauntered into the great room, made a quick tour around...and then went right back out. She enjoyed her breakfast, and then went about her 'rounds' in the back garden, usually ending up under the row of pines where she liked to spend the day now, soaking up any sunshine that filtered through mother nature's protective cover. She'd recline on a thick bed of pine needles beneath the pine boughs that sheltered from the winds. Or – she could be found taking advantage of the 'cat's nest' view atop the garden shed to survey this new 'empire' of hers. And I imagine she weighed in her kitty processes of mind, if this, out of all the places in the neighborhood, was somewhere she truly wanted to stay.

Now, each day, Salinka came in at breakfast, made a round tour of the great room, sometimes spending a bit more time investigating different points and pieces of furniture...and definitely checking out the other furry in-house residents, who watched with some *very* indignant awe as she sauntered through THEIR environs! But interestingly, no one hissed, no one challenged...and they even approached her from time to time, to be warded off on her part with a hefty *HISSssss!* Of course, I was very careful not to allow contact between her and my other residents. She had not been vetted and I had to be wary of fleas as well.

Before spring arrived officially, Salinka had decided she would stay inside for a bit. She allowed me to pick her up for short periods of time, and I managed to get her to the vet.

She found a nook up high on the cat tree...and surveyed the others from above. After breakfast, she would want to go out, and return for dinner. Within a few weeks, Salinka was staying inside for the night!

She had been surveilling me, the other furry residents and the premises to see if they met her specific standards. Despite the hard life she led, this was a cat that deeply cherished freedom, perhaps due to her very obvious fear of humans. Yet she seemed to understand that time was ticking, and that the hardy outdoor habits that she had practiced now for a few years at least, might not continue on. She seemed very interested in finding a real 'home' -- one that gave her inside comfort, good food, security and safety, while allowing her the freedom to also safely enjoy the wonders of mother nature she so coveted. And she definitely showed she was interested in exchanging affection, but definitely on her terms.

Salinka eventually warmed up to more petting, and one day, as I sat reading the paper...she climbed up next to me and cast her big, gorgeous orbs upwards to look me straight in the eye! I reached out to stroke her...and she started to purr! And then, to my astonishment, she stretched out beside me...and put her paw up on my lap!

This girl, who defended her freedom, her individuality, was not about to allow anyone to make a decision for her. She was going to decide where and how she wanted to live her days...and despite all the other 'competition' she had from our other residents, she decided to stay with us. Salinka had been browsing the neighborhood, 'shopping' for her own new home over these years! Her months of observation and investigation had a purpose it seems!

And she remains with us today. Fortunately, the vet check turned up NO diseases! I was absolutely astounded - and ecstatically grateful. This young, slinky cat now crawls atop my chest, kneads my belly to make a 'nest'...and settles in for nightly repose before my own bedtime. This formerly **strictly aloof** little luvbug, who rejected more than a few strokes and ear scratches for months on end...and would never come when she was called, but remained where she wanted to be, observing all of us -- this lovely furball now won't allow a day to go by without a special amount of attention. If she doesn't sprawl full length out on me as we watch TV, I'll know something is wrong!

An evolution from ' Alley-Cat Aloof' to 'Kitty-Clinger!'

Salinka is clearly jealous of other cats claiming a hug or snuggle. When other resident cats are witnessed with some 'loving' going on, she watches intently, and within a few minutes, exits her perch and finds her special spot on my already over-kneaded person!

Lessons from a Feline Friend

Salinka is exemplary of much of what I have learned and witnessed from the many, many little furry hearts I've shared lives with in my rescue and hospice sanctuary.

Some people love to believe the saying *'dumb animals.'* They take the phrase literally, as well as the biblical *'dominion over animals'* and feel some inborn 'right' to decide the fate of other lives. Valid lives that cannot speak our tongue or stand up for themselves or pass laws for themselves. Far too many feel that such lives are theirs to dominate. To harm or dispose of as they so choose...simply because they're bigger. Simply because they can.

'Dominion' harbors a far different perspective in my view with these creatures. They, too, have rights, and my time with these remarkable creatures of mother nature has proven to me that 'dominion' impresses upon us not the *'right'* to do with them as we please, but rather our creation-given *responsibility*, as sentient beings higher up the chain, to protect, nurture and take responsibility for their welfare as well as our own. Not, as is too often practiced, to get rid of them by whatever means when they are inconvenient to our selfish desires. Or when they are simply being cats, trying simply to survive -- hungry, scared, alone and possibly wounded or dying.

Domesticated cats cannot always rely on wild instincts, which don't work well in the city nor in the country anyway. Far too many dangers out there. They may possibly have never been taught how to cope in 'natural' ways, which, nonetheless, are irrelevant amidst the many dangers of the streets or fields, in an increasingly crowded and hostile world of other animals, traffic, modern hazards, environmental toxins and people.

Some folks perpetuate the incredible myth that animals have no feelings, that they don't feel pain like we do, physically or emotionally. That they don't really have the ability to 'love' us, but respond only to food and nothing more. Hogwash. I have nurtured many dozens of cats and I know differently. An ailing cat hides its pain out of instinct for survival. While they certainly do respond to the care given, they go beyond. Each cat has its own distinct personality, its own likes and dislikes. And their own amazing innate intelligence, measurable not from our abilities but from theirs.

They learn to study us, our language and figure out how to communicate. And many of them respond to sadness, a down day and grief in remarkable ways. I have witnessed special cuddles and snuggles up next to me or in my lap on days when I surely was not in a happy state. The least we can do is make a return effort to understand and respect these wonderful creatures and their innate rights, along with not expecting them to be 'people' when we invite them into our homes. And also when we do not.

If we simply learn to allow for their needs in ways that also respect ours and to think ahead to guide the expression of their innate behaviors in ways acceptable as members of a family, there is peaceful coexistence...and likely much, much more (*i.e., provide appropriate scratching posts in our homes to accommodate their biological need to scratch – and thus save the furnishings*).

Cats can be trained. With patience -- and care to avoid instilling bad habits in them from the beginning with our own behavior (which makes the 'undoing' far more difficult), most cats can be taught to be exemplary members of the household. They do want to please us. In all the years of my sanctuary care duties, I have never come across a cat that remained totally aloof by not wanting my affection, approval and praise. They may start out that way for sure, influenced by a hard life or cruel treatment they have received, but they all have come around to one degree or another. Sadly, many feral cats may never come around, since they were never socialized to people at an early enough age. Or they may have insurmountable fears due to abuses from humankind.

I've witnessed that cats do feel jealousy, just as we humans can. They respond to kindness and caring. And they respond in kind. They show affection and yes, love. So many folks don't want to believe it. And cats can show gratitude, each in their own way.

I could tell stories of different ways my rescues decide to 'contribute' to the household. One of my rescues, amusingly, has taken upon herself 'police duties,' providing a swift bat to any resident that might decide to break one of the 'house rules.' Should one of them decide to impose themselves in another cat's dinner dish, she is there to let them know otherwise! If I scold another resident for something, she is immediately there to lend her feline backup to my commands with a loud vocal, sometimes followed by a mini-swat at the perpetrator. She relishes her role and needs her own 'guidance' on this issue from time to time.

Cats can understand when you say you are sorry. I've inadvertently stepped on the tail or toes of a few who got underfoot. Taking a moment to pet them, look them in the eyes and gently touch the area you hurt and say, *"Aww...I'm sorry,"* almost always has gotten me a lick or head rub. And unconditional forgiveness. Not doing so leaves them with a hurt look in their eyes that is very telling. I've seen others ignore their cats when they inadvertently hurt their little charges. When such behavioral dismissal was perpetuated, the cats started to avoid their human companions with time. They became more 'aloof.' Cats understand respect and respond to it.

Cats, and I will wager you with confidence, all animals, as living creatures, relate to our attempts to understand their needs if given time. It doesn't mean we should try to tame wildlife, but it does show to me that they deserve our utmost respect for them and their needs. Living creatures experience emotions. Wild animals have been witnessed grieving losses of their family members. They understand dissatisfaction from their peers. Simply because we haven't personally witnessed or understand their behaviors - or maybe don't care - doesn't change the facts. Others have studied the realm of animals around the world, and the evidence is there if we look. Or experience it for yourself through the nurture and care of a chosen 'pet,' preferably a forgotten, ailing, lost or homeless one, regardless of species. Or care for a dying, lonely waif and see them through their final breath. Your heart – and insight – will never be the same.

I've learned some of the language of my little 'charges.' Their different 'meows' and tones for different things they want. And each cat has its own way of expressing its needs. I've also identified different telling 'trills' of some of my luvbugs, who answer a question or sing-song their satisfaction or disapproval about any matter at hand.

For so long, Salinka didn't make a sound. Except a loud protest when she'd had enough touching. She didn't even purr when I stroked her, although you could tell she enjoyed it. She was still too wary to trust, I think. Still too emotionally damaged, perhaps, to openly show her feelings. Perhaps, like us, she protected herself from additional disappointment or heartbreak if, after exposing her heart to trust, she was let down once again? Or worse.

Now... she 'talks' to me regularly...and oh boy...does she have a voice as unique as her markings! You KNOW when Salinka speaks up!

She gives so much joy with her ways and antics and usually wants to stay indoors nowadays. She has had her fill of the hard outdoor street life, despite the freedom she felt. After at least two years of seeing her in the neighborhood, and another year of visits before she decided to adopt us, Salinka is here to stay.

The only thing that must change is my reference to Salinka as **'she.'**

When Salinka finally trusted me enough to pick her up, she was taken to the vet and found to be a "HE." The vet had to look more than once! She was marked so strategically, that it was hard to tell with a quick glance.

But the name remains Salinka. It's easier to say than' Salinky' or 'Salinkov' -- which I'd considered.

No, Salinka it is. It still fits.

He is the same sweet, yet determined feline, peaceful and loving -- and just as gorgeous as a boy as he was as a girl!

And although it is yet another mouth to feed, more vet bills and more chaos at times, I feel blessed. It's a wonderful feeling to see him safe, thriving and healthy. And the love -- yes love -- that is exchanged is vast reward. And indisputable.

May you, too, be inspired to give your heart to an unfortunate castaway - and experience the special bonds and joys that these loving creatures will give back to you many times over. Yes, there may be some challenges, as with any worthwhile relationship, but their company and natural charm will brighten your days. And the Love that grows between you and your furry feline family members will enrich your daily journey for a Lifetime.

May you find your own delightful version of Salinka to love and enjoy. Or maybe, one or more will find *you!*

Here in our special sanctuary, with his housemates, Salinka has a safe, happy and loving home - forever. His 'shopping days' are done. Salinka has come 'home.' Amen.

Young Salinka surveils the garden scene in our Sanctuary, atop his favorite perch in the cold.

>^..^<

"Never, never be afraid to do what's right, especially if the well being of a person or animal is at stake. Society's punishments are small compared to the wounds we inflict on our soul when we look the other way." ~ Martin Luther King, Jr.

Cateline Beem has served as official *'TopCat'* in her private Sanctuary for more than 20 years, providing safe, loving refuge and a forever home to multiple dozens of homeless, sick, injured, abused, unwanted or dying cats and kittens.

Feline Treatment.net - Alternative and Conventional Cat Care, Health and Behavior **(http://FelineTreatment.net)**

Cat Zone - Cat articles, FREE resources, help and information about all things C A T S **(http://Cats.YouniqueSolutions.com)**

FREE Cat Food Recipes! *'Cat Cuisine from your Kitchen'* - Find Peace of Mind from all the pet food recalls! Get YOUR Free copy! **(http://youniquesolutions.com/su/Ccfkcrg.html)**

In addition to her Cat sites, discover a variety of additional Topics at the 'Sister Sites' of *Younique Solutions.com* - The **PORTAL** to various *Content Zones*, community participation opportunities and some special Boutiques! And MUCH MORE to come! (http://YouniqueSolutions.com)

Other books by R.J. Peters, available at Amazon.com, or directly from the author at the following websites:

How to Make Your Cat Adore You

>   www. TheProblemCat. com

7 Steps to 9 Lives

>   www. 7Stepsto9Lives .com

Moving With Pets

>   www. TheProblemCat. com/letsmove/

Alternative Healing Choices

>   www. AlternativeHealingChoices. com/book/

Cat Quotes

Bonus Section

You may have noticed the quotes at the end of each story. I tried to select one that seemed most relevant to each tale, and I sifted through quite a lot in my quest. Some of these stories could use more than one quote, but I settled on the one I thought was best. I enjoyed reading them and decided to share with you the list I assembled for your enjoyment.

"If a homeless cat could talk, it would probably say, 'Give me shelter, food, companionship and love, and I will be yours for life!" - Susan Easterly

"The key to a successful new relationship between a cat and human is patience." - Susan Easterly

"Chances are that a man who can nuzzle a kitten is also open and caring in other facets of his life." - Barbara L. Diamond

Cats may, indeed, be the thinking man's pet--because living with cats certainly keeps you on your toes!" - Barbara L. Diamond

"How nice it is to think that feline dreams, like our own, are painted with creative brush strokes from time to time. Perhaps my cats and I even share the same dream: a world where all kittens are wanted and loved, and where every cat has a safe, warm place to sleep...and to dream." - Barbara L. Diamond

The really great thing about cats is their endless variety. One can pick a cat to fit almost any kind of décor, color scheme, income, personality, or mood. But under the fur, whatever color it may be, there still lies, essentially unchanged, one of the world's free souls." - Eric Gurney

Cat lovers can readily be identified. Their clothes always look old and well used. Their sheets look like bath towels and their bath towels look like a collection of knitting mistakes. - Eric Gurney, How to Live with a Calculating Cat

"The cat does not offer services. The cat offers itself. Of course he wants care and shelter. You don't buy love for nothing. Like all pure creatures, cats are practical." - William S. Burroughs

"Cats are dangerous companions for writers because cat watching is a near-perfect method of writing avoidance." - Dan Greenburg

"For me, one of the pleasures of cats' company is their devotion to bodily comfort." - Sir Compton Mackenzie

People who belong to Siamese cats must make up their minds to do a good deal of waiting upon them." - Compton Mackenzie

"Cats are much like they were when they were first domesticated. They are very independent because they had to be to survive." - Dr. Raymond Hampton

"Are cats lazy? Well, more power to them if they are. Which one of us has not entertained the dream of doing just as he likes, when and how he likes, and as much as he likes?" - Fernand Mery

"With their qualities of cleanliness, discretion, affection, patience, dignity, and courage, how many of us, I ask you, would be capable of becoming cats?" - Fernand Mery, Her Majesty the Cat

God made the cat in order that man might have the pleasure of caressing the lion. - Fernand Mery

"All cats are possessed of a proud spirit, and the surest way to forfeit the esteem of a cat is to treat him as an inferior being." - Michael Joseph

How we behave toward cats here below determines our status in heaven. - Robert A. Heinlein

"Cats, like butterflies, need no excuse." - Robert A. Heinlein

"There is, indeed, no single quality of the cat that man could not emulate to his advantage." - Carl Van Vechten

"Artists like cats; soldiers like dogs." - Desmond Morris

"My cat speaks sign language with her tail." - Robert A. Stern

"Among animals, cats are the top-hatted, frock-coated statesmen going about their affairs at their own pace." - Robert A. Stern

"There are two means of refuge from the miseries of life: music and cats." - Albert Schweitzer

Cats seem to go on the principle that it never does any harm to ask for what you want. - Joseph Wood Krutch

Like a graceful vase, a cat, even when motionless, seems to flow. - George F. Will

The phrase "domestic cat" is an oxymoron. - George F. Will

A meow massages the heart. - Stuart McMillan

If a cat does something, we call it instinct; if we do the same thing, for the same reason, we call it intelligence. - Will Cuppy

There's no need for a piece of sculpture in a home that has a cat. - Wesley Bates

Cats do not have to be shown how to have a good time, for they are unfailing ingenious in that respect. - James Mason

Meow is like aloha - it can mean anything. - Hank Ketchum

As every cat owner knows, nobody owns a cat. - Ellen Perry Berkeley

You can't own a cat. The best you can do is be partners. - Sir Harry Swanson

Cats know how to obtain food without labor, shelter without confinement, and love without penalties. - W. L. George

We cannot without becoming cats, perfectly understand the cat mind. - St. George Mivart

Two things are aesthetically perfect in the world - the clock and the cat. - Emile Auguste Chartier

Even the stupidest cat seems to know more than any dog. - Eleanor Clark

Kittens are born with their eyes shut. They open them in about six days, take a look around, then close them again for the better part of their lives. - Stephen Baker

Most beds sleep up to six cats. Ten cats without the owner. - Stephen Baker

By associating with the cat, one only risks becoming richer. - Colette

There are no ordinary cats. - Colette

Our perfect companions never have fewer than four feet. - Colette

"I am indebted to the species of the cat for a particular kind of honorable deceit, for a great control over myself, for characteristic aversion to brutal sounds, and for the need to keep silent for long periods of time." - Colette

A cat pours his body on the floor like water. It is restful just to see him. - William Lyon Phelps

There are few things in life more heartwarming than to be welcomed by a cat. - Tay Hohoff

The ideal of calm exists in a sitting cat. - Jules Reynard

Most cats, when they are Out want to be In, and vice versa, and often simultaneously. - Louis F. Camuti, DVM

Way down deep, we're all motivated by the same urges. Cats have the courage to live by them. - Jim Davis

Her function is to sit and be admired. - Georgina Strickland Gates

I believe cats to be spirits come to earth. A cat, I am sure, could walk on a cloud without coming through. - Jules Verne

There is no more intrepid explorer than a kitten. - Jules Champfleury

A kitten is the delight of the household; all day long a comedy is played out by an incomparable actor. - Champfleury

One of the oldest human needs is having someone to wonder where you are when you don't come home at night. - Margaret Mead

"If you are worthy of its affection, a cat will be your friend, but never your slave."- Theophile Gautier

Cats are a mysterious kind of folk. There is more passing in their minds than we are aware of." - Sir Walter Scott

"Cats are a tonic, they are a laugh, they are a cuddle, they are at least pretty just about all of the time and beautiful some of the time."- Roger Caras

"Cats don't like change without their consent." - Roger A. Caras

"The cat seldom interferes with other people's rights. His intelligence keeps him from doing many of the fool things that complicate life." - Carl Van Vechten

"An ordinary kitten will ask more questions than any five year old." - Carl Van Vechten

"Even overweight, cats instinctively know the cardinal rule: when fat, arrange yourself in slim poses." - John Weitz

"People that hate cats will come back as mice in their next life." - Faith Resnick

"Managing senior programmers is like herding cats." - Dave Platt

"Cats are glorious creatures ~ who must on no accounts be underestimated...Their eyes are fathomless depths of cat-world mysteries. - Lesley Anne Ivory (from Glorious Cats, The Paintings of Lesley Anne Ivory)

"I put down my book, The Meaning of Zen, and see the cat smiling into her fur as she delicately combs it with her rough pink tongue.Cat, I would lend you this book to study but it appears you have already read it.She looks up and gives me her full gaze.Don't be ridiculous, she purrs, I wrote it. - from "Miao" by Dilys Laing

"Cats are rather delicate creatures and they are subject to a lot of ailments, but I never heard of one who suffered from insomnia." - Joseph Wood Crutch

"You cannot look at a sleeping cat and feel tense." - Jane Pauley

"There is the little matter of disposal of droppings in which the cat is far ahead of its rivals. The dog is somehow thrilled by what he or any of his friends have produced, hates to leave it, adores smelling it, and sometimes eats it...The cat covers it up if he can..." - Paul Gallico

"The cat has too much spirit to have no heart" - Ernest Menaul

"The problem with cats is that they get the same exact look whether they see a moth or an axe murderer." - Paula Poundstone

"The cat could very well be man's best friend but would never stoop to admitting it." - Doug Larson

"You may own a cat, but cannot govern one." - Kate Sanborn

"It always gives me a shiver when I see a cat seeing what I can't see." - Eleanor Farjeon

"Of all domestic animals the cat is the most expressive. His face is capable of showing a wide range of expressions. His tail is a mirror of his mind. His gracefulness is surpassed only by his agility. And, along with all these, he has a sense of humor." - Walter Chandoha

"A dog is like a liberal, he wants to please everybody. A cat doesn't really need to know that everybody loves him." - William Kunstler

"It is remarkable, in cats, that the outer life they reveal to their masters is one of perpetual boredom." – Robley Wilson, Jr.

"Two cats can live as cheaply as one, and their owner has twice as much fun." - Lloyd Alexander

"There is no cat 'language.' Painful as it is for us to admit, they don't need one." - Barbara Holland

"A catless writer is almost inconceivable. It's a perverse taste, really, since it would be easier to write with a herd of buffalo in the room than even one cat; they make nests in the notes and bite the end of the pen and walk on the typewriter keys." - Barbara Holland

"Time spent with cats is never wasted." - May Sarton

"The furry little buggers [cats] are just deep, deep wells you throw your emotions into." - Bruce Schimmel

"Cats can work out mathematically the exact place to sit that will cause the most inconvenience."- Pam Brown

"Cats have an infallible understanding of total concentration--and get between you and it."- Arthur Bridges

"A kitten is so flexible that she is almost double; the hind parts are equivalent to another kitten with which the forepart plays. She does not discover that her tail belongs to her until you tread on it."- Henry David Thoreau

"If the pull of the outside world is strong, there is also a pull towards the human. The cat may disappear on its own errands, but sooner or later, it returns once again for a little while, to greet us with its own type of love. Independent as they are, cats find more than pleasure in our company."- Lloyd Alexander

"Cats were put into the world to disprove the dogma that all things were created to serve man."- Paul Gray

"Cat said, 'I am not a friend, and I am not a Servant. I am the Cat who walks by himself, and I wish to come into your Cave.'" - Rudyard Kipling, from the "Just-So Stories"

To err is human, to purr is feline. - Robert Byrne

The ideal of calm exists in a sitting cat. - Jules Reynard

If cats could talk, they wouldn't. - Nan Porter

"Another cat? Perhaps. For love there is also a season; its seeds must be resown. But a family cat is not replaceable like a wornout coat or a set of tires. Each new kitten becomes its own cat, and none is repeated. I am four cats old, measuring out my life in friends that have succeeded but not replaced one another." - Irving Townsend

"No one shall deny me my own conclusions, nor my cat her reflective purr." - Irving Townsend

"A kitten is chiefly remarkable for rushing about like mad at nothing whatever, and generally stopping before it gets there." - Agnes Repplier

It is impossible for a lover of cats to banish these alert, gentle, and discriminating little friends, who give us just enough of their regard and complaisance to make us hunger for more. - Agnes Repplier

"The domestic cat seems to have greater confidence in itself than in anyone else." - Lawrence N. Johnson

"Any household with at least one feline member has no need for an alarm clock." - Louise A. Belcher

"Some animals are secretive; some are shy. A cat is private." - Leonard Michaels

"He has become a much better cat than I have a person. With his gentle urgings, he made me realize that life doesn't end just because one has a few obstacles to overcome." - Mary F. Graf

"In reality, cats are probably better off remaining indoors and sending out their humans to deal with the outside world."
- Dr. Phyllis Sherman Raschke

"I would gladly change places with any of my cats." - George Ney

"I think I'll come back as a cat." - George Ney

"Most cats are not shy about letting their people know what they want." - Karen Duprey

"Many cats simply pounce to their own drummers." - Karen Duprey

"A cat's name may tell you more about its owners than it does about the cat." - Linda W. Lewis

"The cat does not negotiate with the mouse." - Robert K. Massie

"Cats often devise their own sets of rules that they think we should live by, and they may be quick to chastise us if we fail to adhere to these rules!" - Margaret Reister, D.V.M.

"The constant challenge to decipher feline behavior is perhaps one of the most fascinating qualities of owning a cat." - Carole Wilbourn

"One of the quickest ways to a cat's brain is through its stomach." - Ian Dunbar, Ph.D.

"A cat...would check to see if you brought anything to eat, and if not, would turn and walk away, tail held high." - Mike Deupree

"When a cat chooses to be friendly, it's a big deal, because a cat is picky." - Mike Deupree

"Each one of our cats is a distinct, four-footed little person with an individual personality." - Ira B. Rubin

"The cat lets Man support her. But unlike the dog, she is no handlicker. Furthermore, unlike Man's other great good friend, the horse, the cat is no sweating serf of Man. The only labor she condescends to perform is to catch mice and rats, and that's fun." - Vance Packard

Four little Persians, but only one looked in my direction. I extended a tentative finger and two soft paws clung to it. There was a contented sound of purring, I suspect on both our parts. - George Frredley

Because of our willingness to accept cats as superhuman creatures, they are the ideal animals with which to work creatively. - Roni Schotter

His friendship is not easily won but it is something worth having. - Michael Joseph

In Egypt, the cats...afford evidence that animal nature is not altogether intractable, but that when well-treated they are good at remembering kindness. - Aelian

The cat is the only animal which accepts the comforts but rejects the bondage of domesticity. - Georges Louis Leclerc de Buffon

Curiosity is the very basis of education and if you tell me that curiosity killed the cat, I say only the cat died nobly. - Arnold Edinborough

"Those who'll play with cats must expect to be scratched."- Cervantes

"To respect the cat is the beginning of the aesthetic sense." - Erasmus Darwin

"When all candles be out, all cats be gray." - John Heywood

Cat: A pygmy lion who loves mice, hates dogs, and patronizes human beings. - Oliver Herford

If there is one spot of sun spilling onto the floor, a cat will find it and soak it up. - Joan Asper McIntosh

For every house is incomplete without him, and a blessing is lacking in the spirit. - Christopher Smart

Cats never strike a pose that isn't photogenic. - Lillian Jackson Braun

There is nothing in the animal world, to my mind, more delightful than grown cats at play. They are so swift and light and graceful, so subtle and designing, and yet so richly comical. - Monica Edwards

Cats, no less liquid than their shadows, offer no angles to the wind. They slip, diminished, neat, through loopholes less than themselves. - A. S. J. Tessimond

Cats possess so many of the same qualities as some people that it is often hard to tell the people and the cats apart. - P. J. O'Rourke

One of the ways in which cats show happiness is by sleeping. Cleveland Amory

No tame animal has lost less of its native dignity or maintained more if its ancient reserve. The domestic cat might rebel tomorrow. - William Conway

Animals are such agreeable friends - they ask no questions, they pass no criticisms. - George Eliot

Confront a child, a puppy, and a kitten with sudden danger; the child will turn instinctively for assistance, the puppy will grovel in abject submission, the kitten will brace its tiny body for a frantic resistance. - Saki

If you want to write, keep cats. - Aldous Huxley

Cats are the tigers of us poor devils. - Theophile Gautier

"We should be careful to get out of an experience only the wisdom that is in it and stop there, lest we be like the cat that sits down on a hot stove-lid. She will never sit down on a hot stove-lid again, and that is well; but also she will never sit down on a cold one anymore." - Mark Twain

"A home without a cat, and a well-fed, well-petted and properly revered cat, may be a perfect home, perhaps; but how can it prove its title?" - Mark Twain

"Of all God's creatures, there is only one that cannot be made slave of the lash. That one is the cat. If man could be crossed with the cat it would improve the man, but it would deteriorate the cat." - Mark Twain

If animals could speak, the dog would be a a blundering outspoken fellow, but the cat would have the rare grace of never saying a word too much. - Mark Twain

"One of the most striking differences between a cat and a lie is that a cat only has nine lives." - Mark Twain

Ignorant people think it is the noise which fighting cats make that is so aggravating, but it ain't so; it is the sickening grammar that they use. - Mark Twain

"Beware of those who dislike cats."- Traditional

Civilization is defined by the presence of cats." - Unknown

"It's really the cat's house - we just pay the mortgage." - Unknown

"There is no snooze button on a cat who wants breakfast." - Unknown

"If you yell at a cat, you're the one who is making a fool of yourself." - Unknown

"A cat sees us as the dogs...A cat sees himself as the human." - Unknown

Purring is an automatic safety valve device for dealing with happiness overflow. - Anonymous

"Until one has loved an animal, part of their soul remains unawakened." - Unknown

"There are many intelligent species in the universe. They are all owned by cats." - Anonymous

The purity of a person's heart can be quickly measured by how they regard cats. - Anonymous

Every life should have nine cats. – Anonymous

All cats are black inside their genes. - Anonymous

If you want to know the character of a man, find out what his cat thinks of him. - Anonymous

"Always turn and look when your cat gazes behind you with that intent look in her eyes. Some day there might actually be something there." - Anonymous

My little grandson is a darling, but he can never take the place of my cats. - Anonymous Grandmother

Never walk barefoot in a house that has cats. – R.J. Peters

If you want your cat to adore you, first you must adore your cat. – R.J. Peters

Notice of Rights

Notice of Liability

15794019R00060

Made in the USA
Charleston, SC
20 November 2012